# Theory for Strings

A Music Theory Workbook

## Violin Book 1

Abigayle Roemer

Cover design by Alex Kuck

ISBN 979-8-9905053-0-8

# Assignments

| Date | Assignment |
|---|---|
| | |
| | |
| | |
| | |
| | |
| | |
| | |
| | |
| | |
| | |
| | |
| | |
| | |
| | |
| | |
| | |

# How to Read Rhythms

**Definition of Rhythm**: Sound patterns made by notes of various lengths

**Definition of Beat**: A steady pulse, like the ticking of a clock

**Definition of Pitch**: How high or low a note sounds

Below is an example of **Musical Notation** - **notes** arranged on a **staff** to show the pitches and rhythms that make up a piece of music.

**Look closer - can you find and circle the following symbols in the music pictured above?**

The vertical lines on the -staff are called **bar lines**

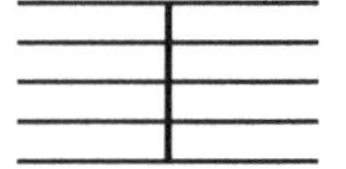

The distance between 2 bar lines is called a **measure**

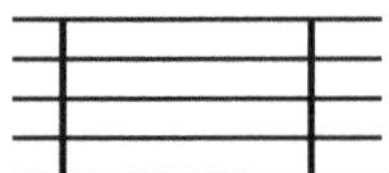

This is called a **time signature** - it shows how many beats are in each measure.
4/4 means there are 4 quarter note beats in each measure.

**There are many different types of notes:**

These different types of notes show you what rhythm to play.

# Practice Drawing Rhythms

How to Draw:

A whole note: Draw an **empty** circle.

A half note: Draw an **empty** circle, add a line going up. The line is called a **stem.**

A quarter note: Draw a **filled** circle, add a **stem.**

An 8th note: Draw a **filled** circle, add a **stem** and a **flag.**

A 16th note: Draw a **filled** circle, add a **stem** and **two flags.**

Draw 8 ______ ______ ______ ______ ______ ______ ______ ______

Draw 8 ______ ______ ______ ______ ______ ______ ______ ______

Draw 8 ______ ______ ______ ______ ______ ______ ______ ______

Draw 8 ______ ______ ______ ______ ______ ______ ______ ______

Draw 8 ______ ______ ______ ______ ______ ______ ______ ______

# Clapping and Counting a Steady Beat

Practice clapping a steady beat: Imagine the ticking of a clock and don't speed up or slow down.

That steady beat, in music, might look like this:

Now practice clapping a steady beat while saying "1 2 3 4" "1 2 3 4" out loud with each clap. You are now counting the beats in each measure.

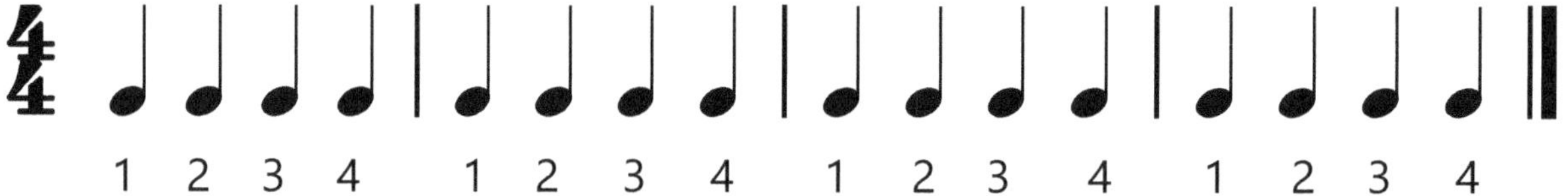


Try clapping the same steady beat while counting the beats silently in your head.
Learning how to do this will help a lot later on!

Try starting at different speeds, but always keep the beat steady once you've started.

Practice drawing a steady beat using quarter notes in the measures below.
Remember there are 4 quarter note beats in every measure!

# Rhythm Pies and Musical Math

In a $\frac{4}{4}$ measure...

A **whole note** gets 4 beats
A **half note** gets 2 beats
A **quarter note** gets 1 beat
An **8th note** gets ½ a beat
A **16th note** gets ¼ a beat

| A whole pie = 1 whole note 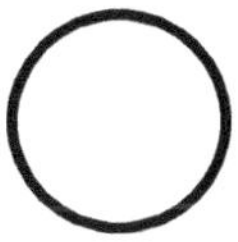 | 1 whole note fits in one measure 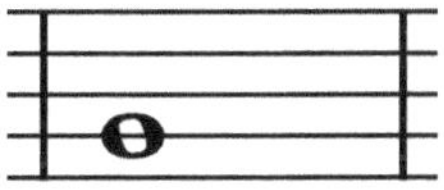 |
|---|---|
| Cut the pie in half, and you get 2 half notes 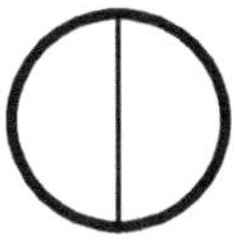 | 2 half notes fit in one measure 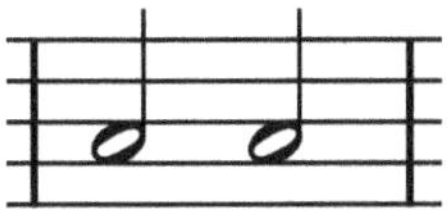 |
| Cut the pie in quarters, and you get 4 quarter notes 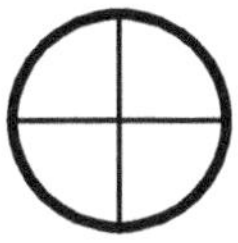 | 4 quarter notes fit in one measure 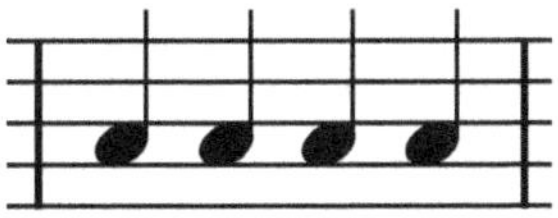 |
| Cut the pie in 8ths, and you get 8 8th notes 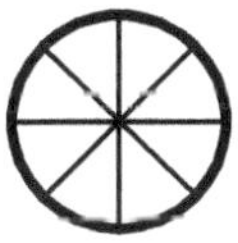 | 8 8th notes fit in one measure 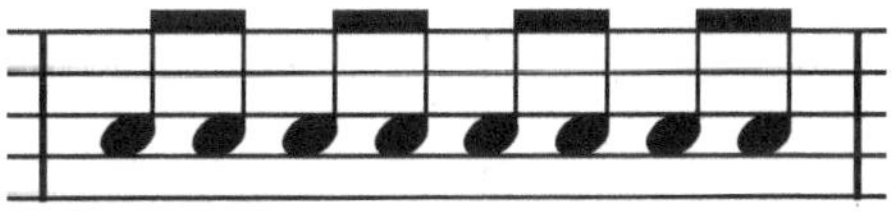 |
| Cut the pie in 16ths, and you get 16 16th notes 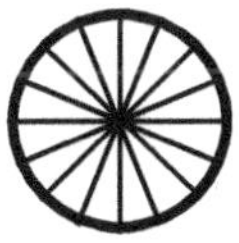 | 16 16th notes fit in one measure 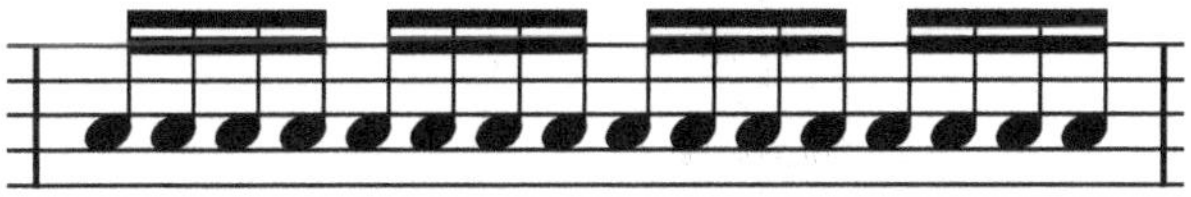 |

Practice Drawing Pies

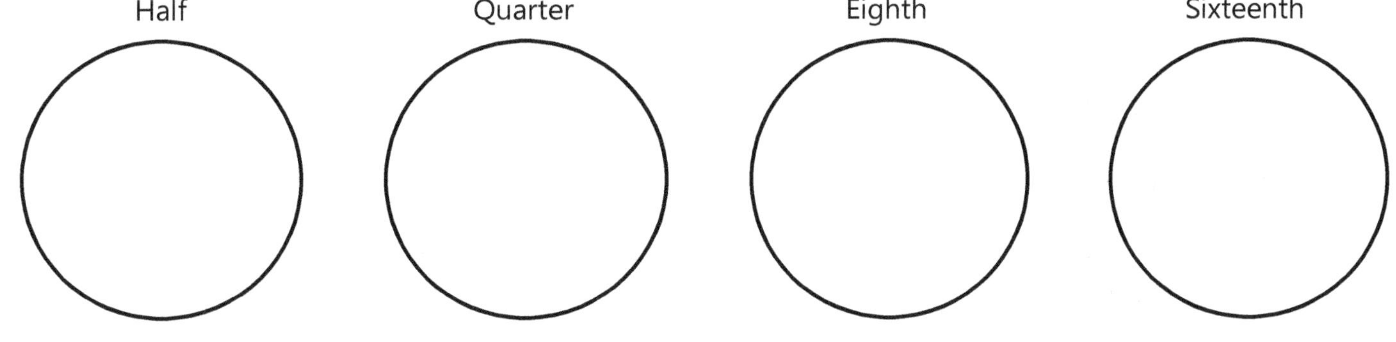

# Practice Rhythm Pies

**Use Rhythm Pies to Answer These Questions**
Example:
Cut the pie in half, then shade the whole pie.

How many half notes are in a whole note? (how many slices are shaded?) 2 ____

1. Cut the pie into quarters, then shade in half the pie.

How many quarter notes are in a half note? ____

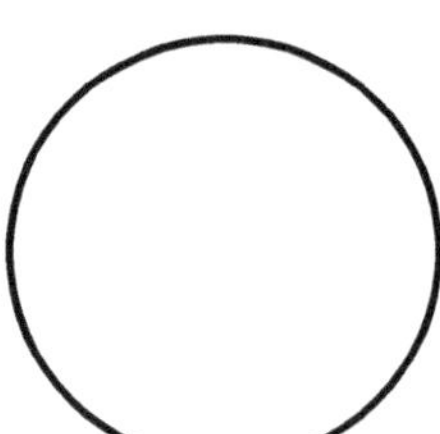

2. Cut the pie into 8ths, then shade in half the pie.

How many 8th notes are in a half note? ____

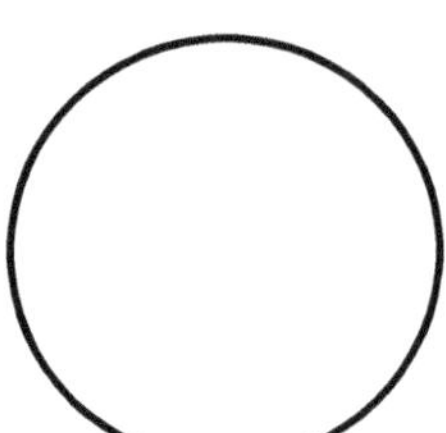

3. Cut the pie into 8ths, then shade in a quarter of the pie.

How many 8th notes are in a quarter note? ____

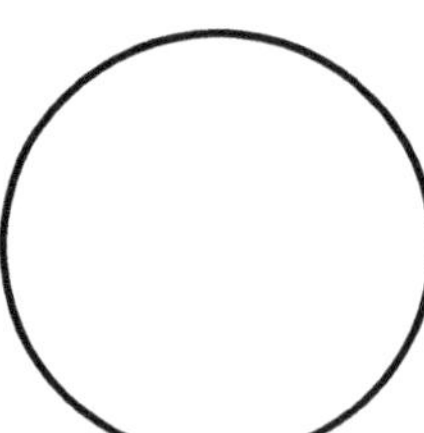

4. Cut the pie into quarters, then shade the whole pie.

How many quarter notes are in a whole note? ____

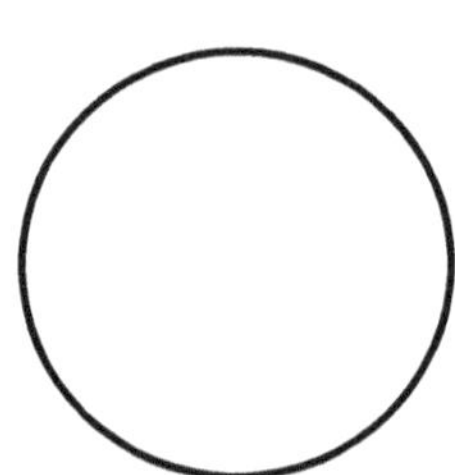

# More Practice

Divide and shade in the pie to answer these questions:

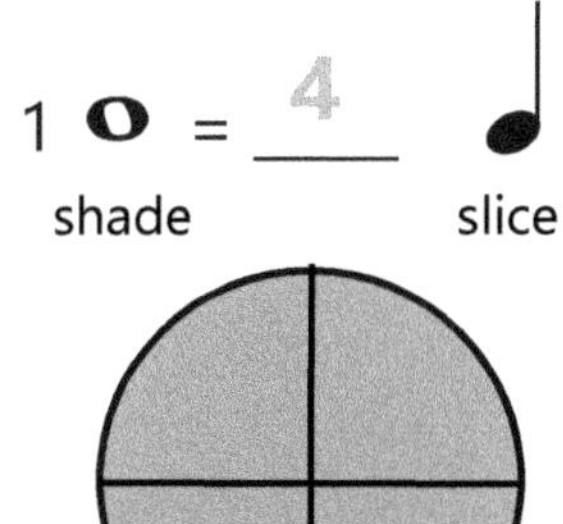


1 = ____

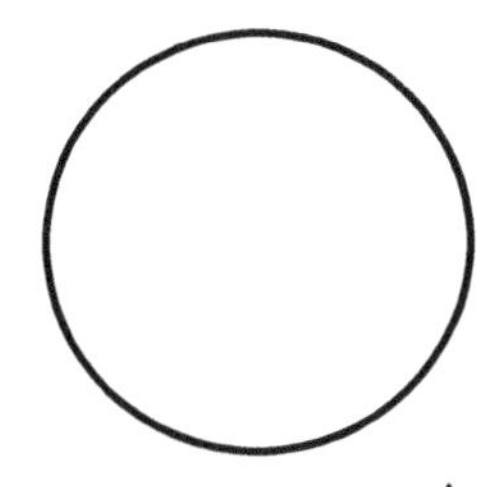

1 = ____

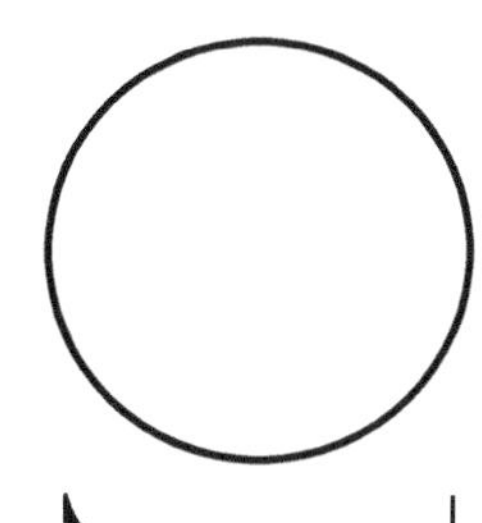

1 = ____

1 = ____

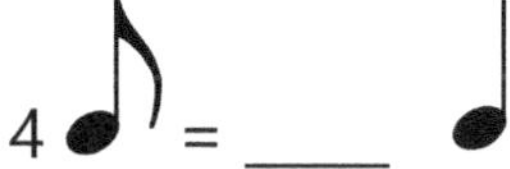


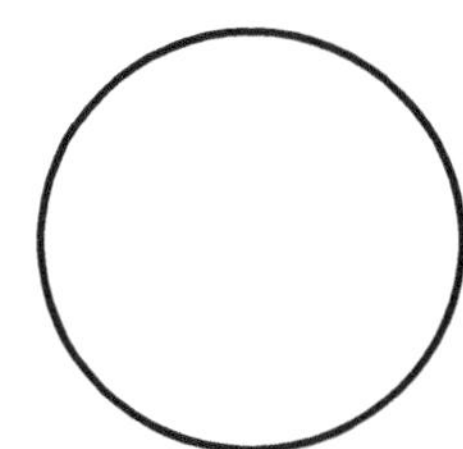

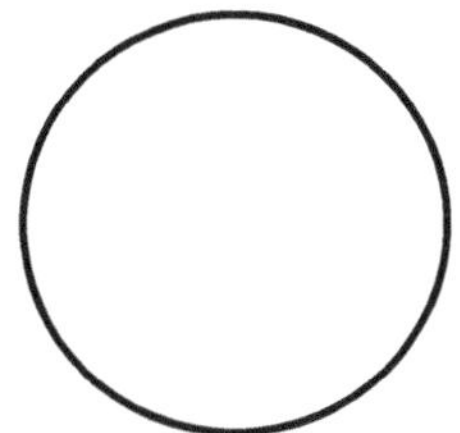

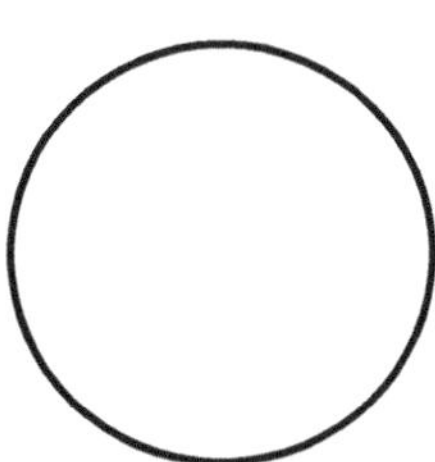

Balance the scale by drawing the correct number of notes:

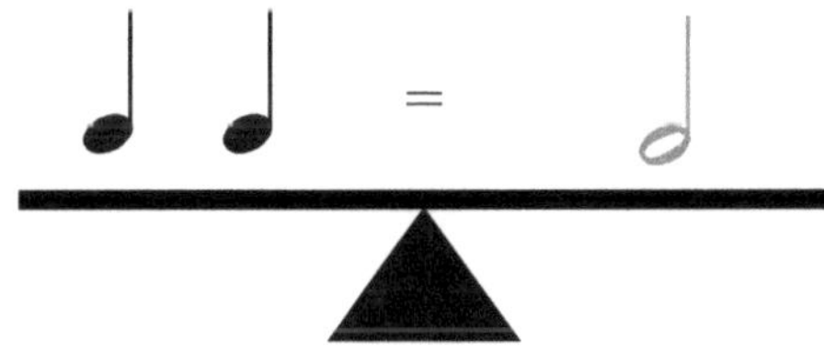

Half Note(s)

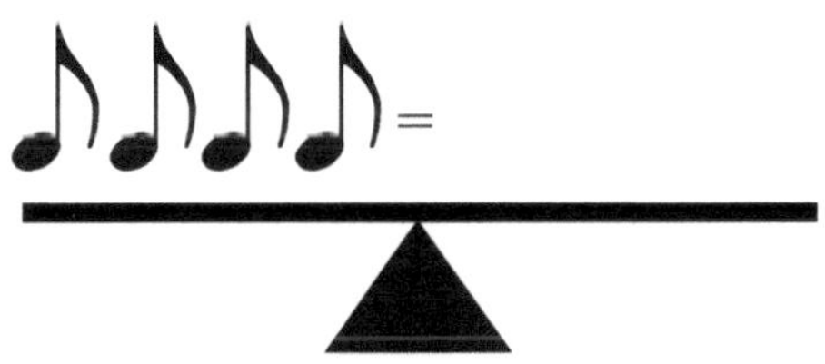

Quarter Note(s)

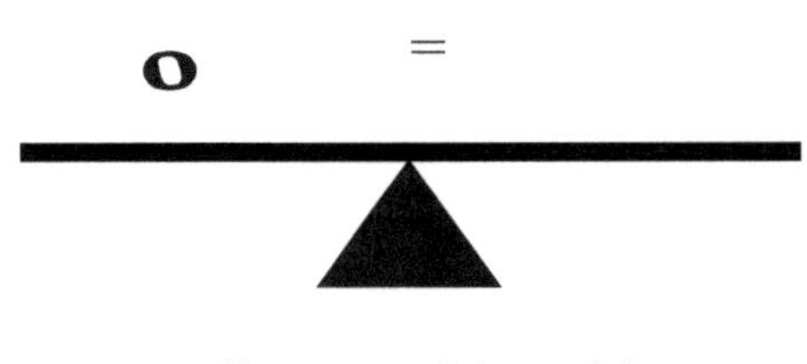

Quarter Note(s)

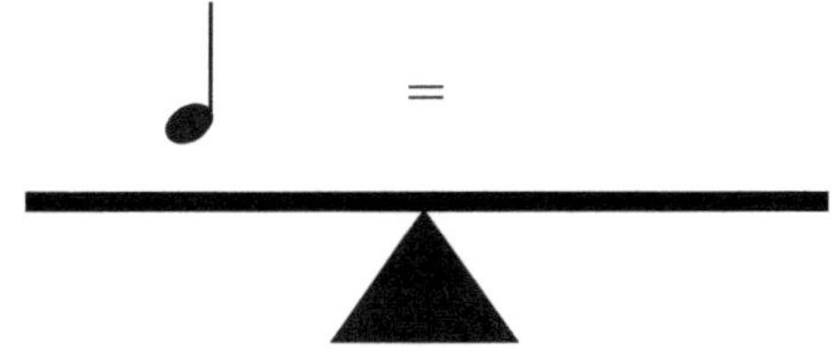

Eighth Note(s)

# Clapping Rhythms

When you clap a rhythm, always count the beats in each measure by saying "1 2 3 4". When you see a number in parentheses ( ), say the beat number out loud but don't clap.

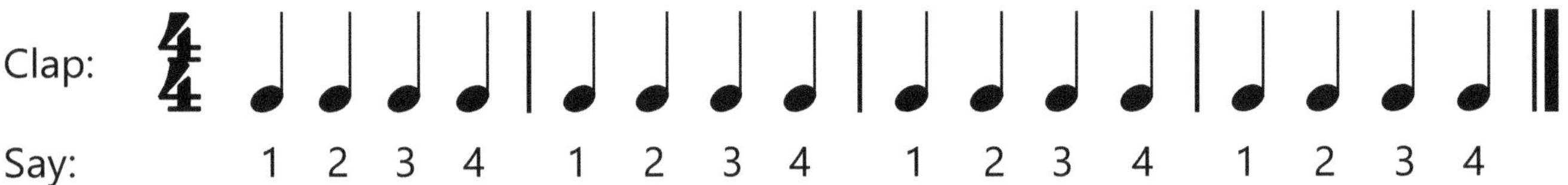


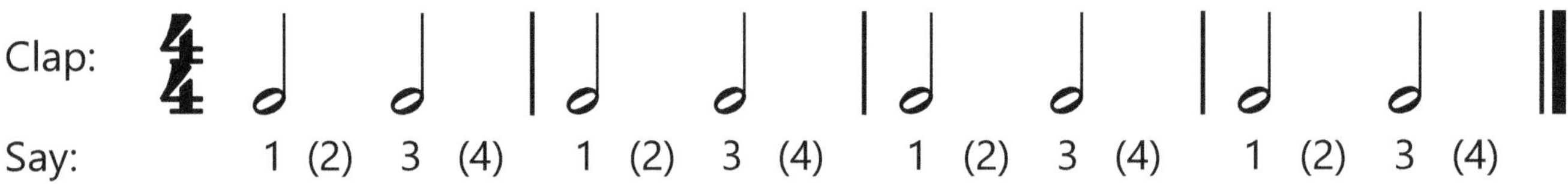


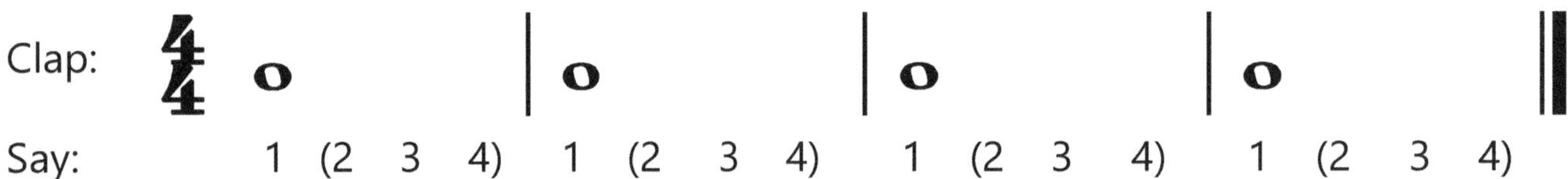


Eventually, practice thinking the beat number in your head instead of saying it out loud.

# Practice Clapping and Counting

Clap the rhythms in the following measures while counting the beats out loud.
Example:

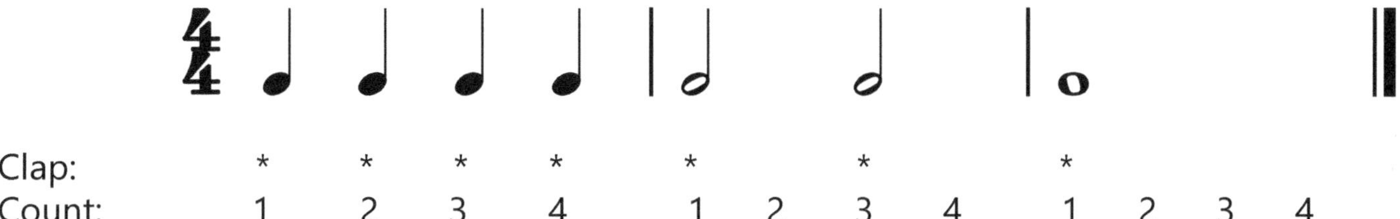

Clap: * * * * * * *
Count: 1 2 3 4 1 2 3 4 1 2 3 4

**Drawing the Beats:**

It can be helpful to draw vertical lines to show where the beats occur. Practice drawing beats in the following measures, then clap the rhythms while counting out loud or silently.

Example:

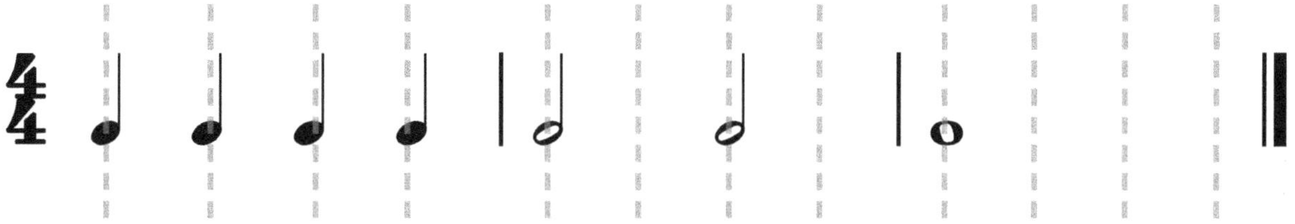

Count: 1 2 3 4 1 2 3 4 1 2 3 4

1.

Count: 1 2 3 4 1 2 3 4 1 2 3 4

2.

Count: 1 2 3 4 1 2 3 4 1 2 3 4

3.

Count: 1 2 3 4 1 2 3 4 1 2 3 4

# Rests

**Rests** are symbols that notate silence.

The whole rest is located just below the fourth line in the staff.

= 4 beats =

Practice drawing whole rests.

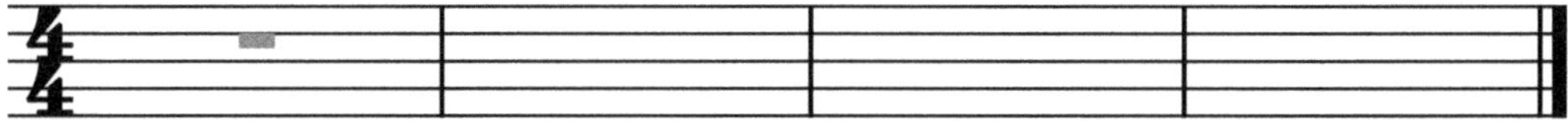

The half rest is located just above  the middle line in the staff.

= 2 beats =

Practice drawing half rests

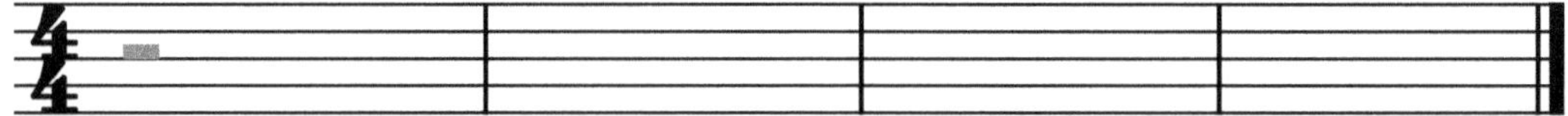

The quarter rest has a unique shape: it can be drawn by writing a slanted "z" with a "c" below it.

= 1 beat =

Practice drawing quarter rests

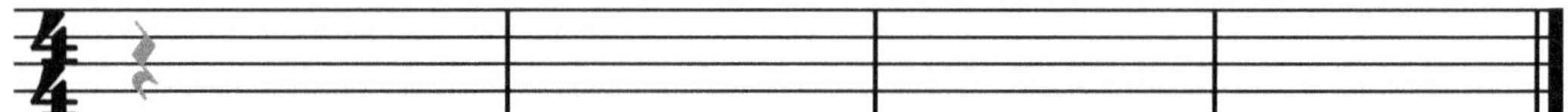

The 8th rest has a flag, similar to the 8th note; it looks like a fancy "7".

= 1/2 beat =

Practice drawing 8th rests

The 16th rest has two flags, similar to the 16th note: it looks like an 8th rest with an extra flag.

= 1/4 beat =

Practice drawing 16th rests

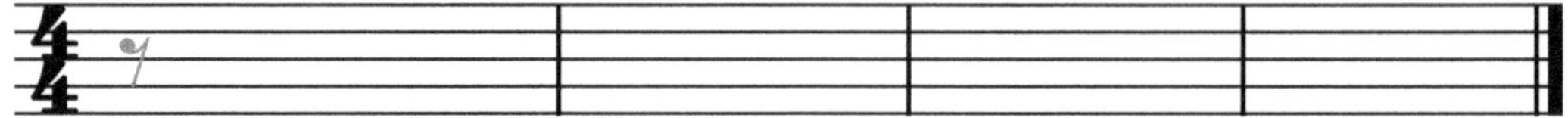

# Counting 8th and 16th notes

8th notes are drawn with a flag.

16th notes are twice as fast as 8th notes, and they are drawn with 2 flags. 

In 4/4 there are two 8th notes in every quarter note beat so they're often drawn like this, connected by a **beam.**

Beams are used to group faster notes together and often show how many fast notes are in one beat.

There are four 16th notes in a quarter note beat, so they're often drawn like this:

When counting 8th notes, say "1 and 2 and 3 and 4 and" so there are two syllables in every beat.

Clap the rhythm above while saying "1 and 2 and 3 and 4 and".

Draw vertical lines through each number to show the beats - **notice how the first note of every beamed group falls on the beat.**

When counting 16th notes, say "1 e and a 2 e and a 3 e and a 4 e and a" so there are four syllables in each beat (pronounced "1 ee and ah").

Clap the rhythm above while saying "1 e and a 2 e and a 3 e and a 4 e and a".

Draw vertical lines through each number to show the beats - notice how the first note of every beamed group falls on the beat.

# Dotted Rhythms

If a note has a dot after it, it's called a **dotted rhythm.**
**A dot lengthens a note by one half.**
For example, if a quarter note is one beat, then a dotted quarter note is 1 and a half beats, which is equal to one quarter note + one 8th note or **three 8th notes.**

A dotted half note is held for **three quarter note** beats.

A dotted 8th note is held for **three 16th notes**, or 3/4 of a quarter note beat.

*note: usually, dotted 8th notes are beamed with a 16th note to complete the beat, so they look like this:

A dotted whole note is held for six quarter note beats, or **three half notes.**

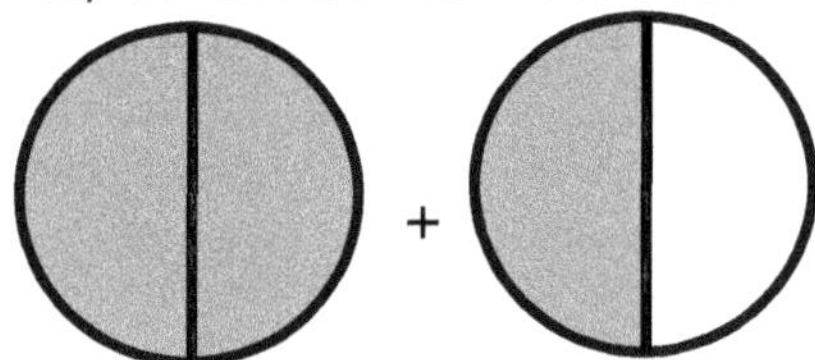


**Notice this pattern:** Usually, a note can be divided into two by the next smallest note. (example: one quarter=two 8ths). A dotted note can be divided into three by the next smallest note (example: one dotted quarter = three 8ths). It can be very helpful to divide by the next smallest note when counting dotted rhythms. This process is called **subdivision.**

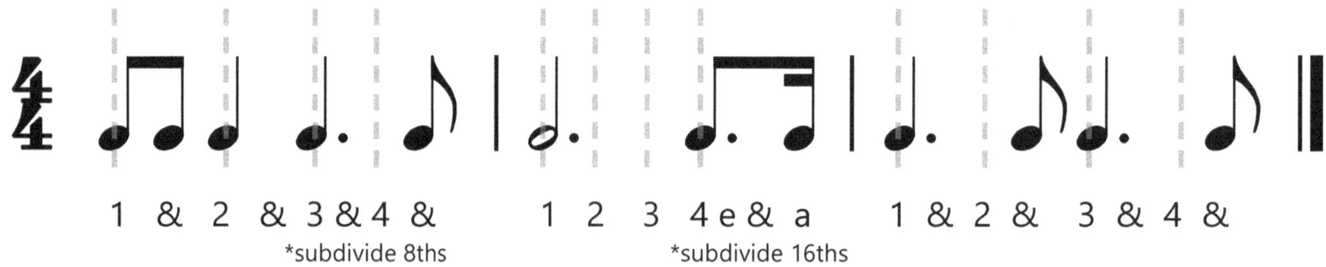

# Clapping Duets

Find a friend, teacher or parent and ask them to clap a steady beat, saying "1 2 3 4"while you clap and say the bottom rhythm. If done correctly, notice how your numbers always match!

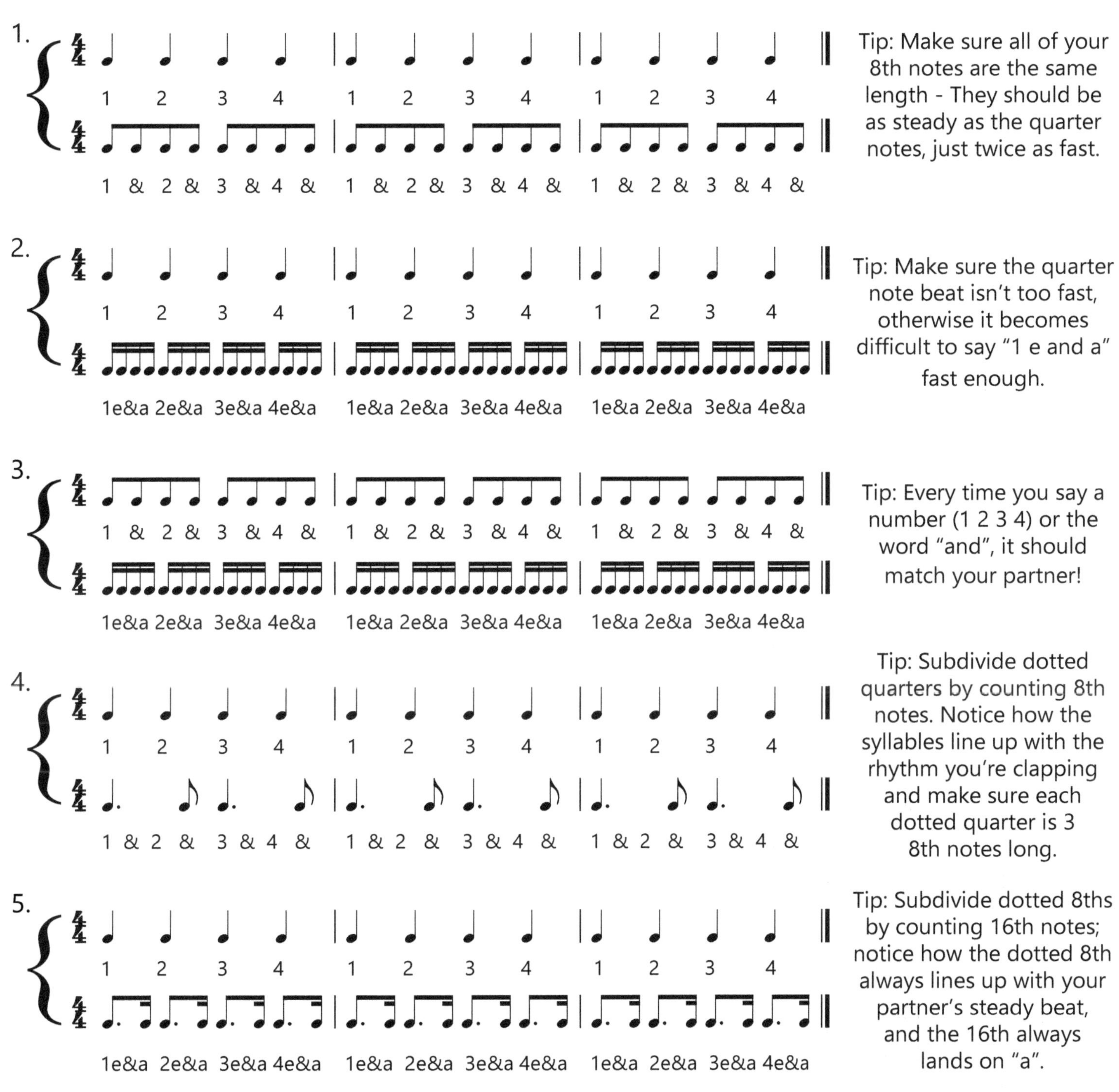


Tip: Make sure all of your 8th notes are the same length - They should be as steady as the quarter notes, just twice as fast.

Tip: Make sure the quarter note beat isn't too fast, otherwise it becomes difficult to say "1 e and a" fast enough.

Tip: Every time you say a number (1 2 3 4) or the word "and", it should match your partner!

Tip: Subdivide dotted quarters by counting 8th notes. Notice how the syllables line up with the rhythm you're clapping and make sure each dotted quarter is 3 8th notes long.

Tip: Subdivide dotted 8ths by counting 16th notes; notice how the dotted 8th always lines up with your partner's steady beat, and the 16th always lands on "a".

# Counting and Playing Rests

Clap when you see a quarter note and say the beat number.
Shrug when you see a quarter rest and say the beat number.

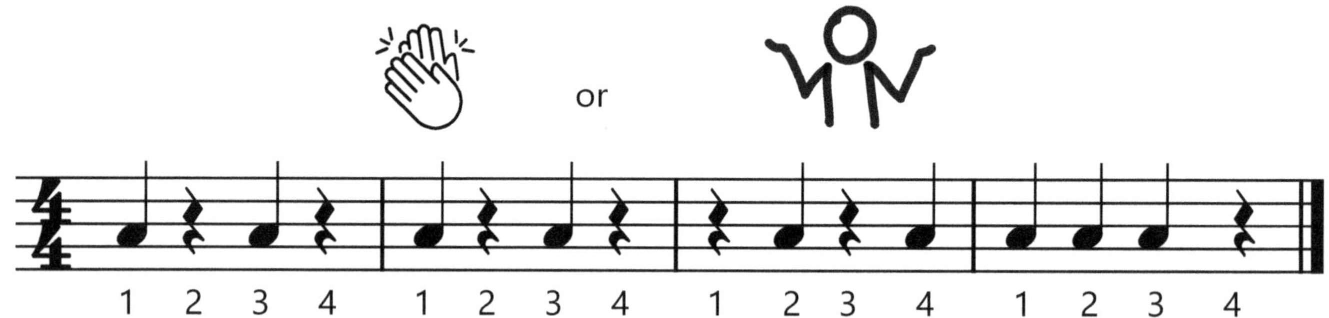


Always keep the quarter note beat steady, whether you're playing or resting!

More Practice...
*Numbers in parentheses should be counted out loud, but not clapped in these exercises.

Try clapping the following rhythms while tapping a steady quarter note beat with your foot (or ask a friend to clap a steady beat, or use a metronome!)

1.

1 2 (3) 4

2.
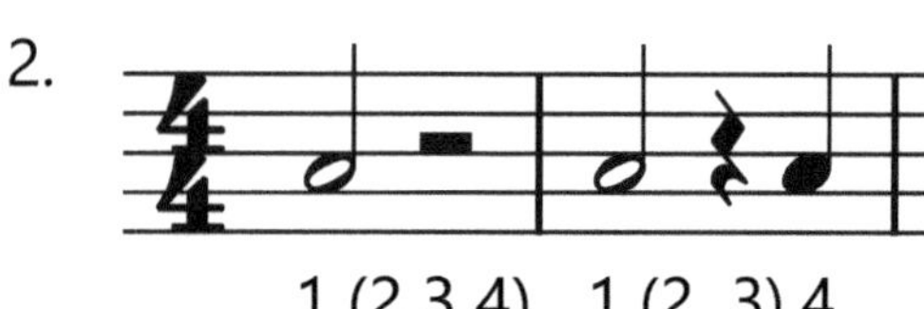
1 (2 3 4) 1 (2 3) 4

3.

1 & (2) & 3 (4)

4.
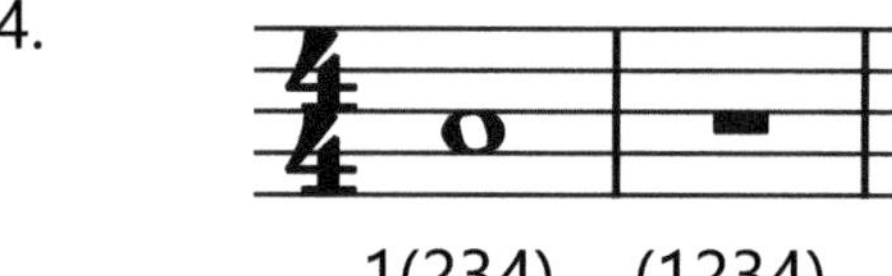
1(234) (1234)

5.

1 (2 3) 4

6.

1 (2) & 3 & (4) &

# Rhythm Quiz

| Name this note or rest: | Draw this note or rest: |
|---|---|
| 𝄽 ____________________ | Whole note: |
| 𝅝 ____________________ | Half rest: |
| ♪ ____________________ | Quarter note: |
| 𝄾 ____________________ | 8th rest: |
| 𝅗𝅥 ____________________ | Four 16th notes (beamed): |

How many beats are in a 𝅝 ______

How many beats are in a 𝄽 ______

How many beats are in a 𝅗𝅥 ______

How many ♪ are in a ♩ ______

How many 𝅘𝅥𝅯 are in a ♩ ______

Fill these measures with the correct number of quarter, half, whole and 8th notes or rests.
Remember to beam 8th notes to show where the beats are.

4/4

♩ 𝅗𝅥 ♪ 𝅝

# How to Read Notes

**Definition of Pitch**: How high or low a note sounds

Notes are placed at different positions on the staff to show how high or low the pitch is.

A staff has 5 lines and 4 spaces

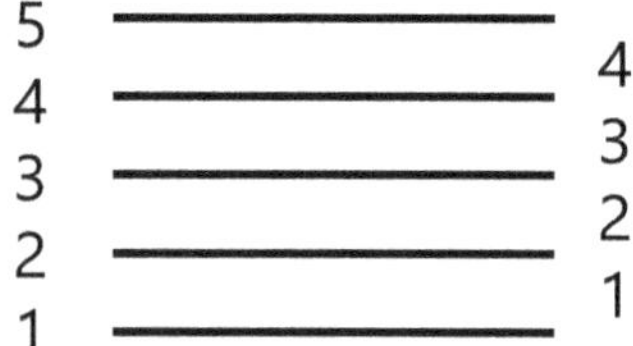


Notes can be placed on lines

Or on spaces

When all the notes are lined up in order, it looks like this:

Which line is this note on? (1=lowest 5=highest)

 ____

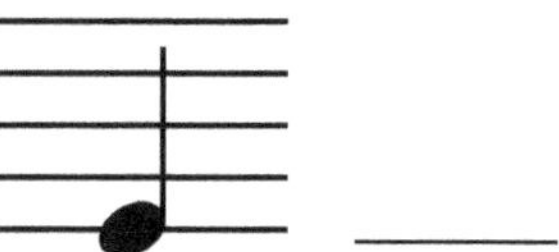 ____

 ____

Which space is this note on (1=lowest 4=highest)

 ____

 ____

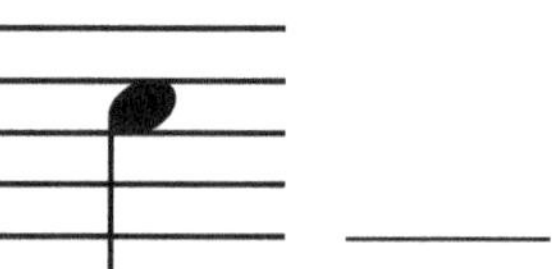 ____

Practice drawing this line note 3 times:

Practice drawing this space note 3 times:

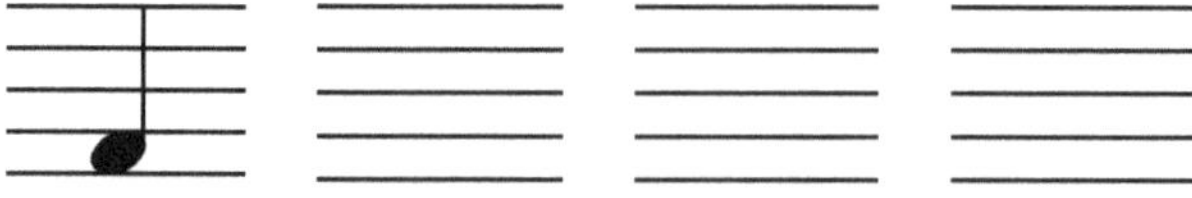

# Musical Alphabet

Every note has a letter name:

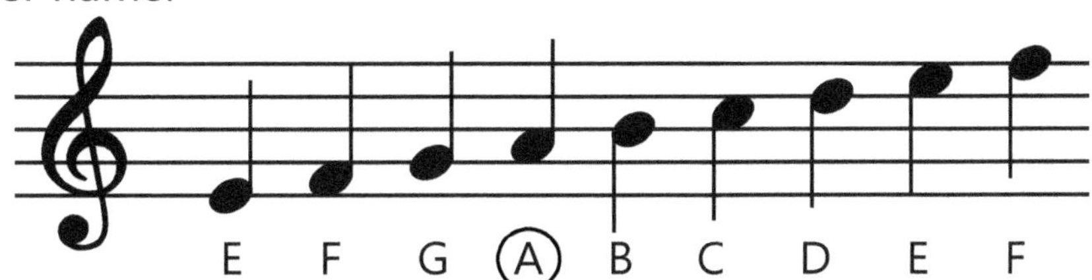


Notice how if you start with the note A (circled above) the notes move up in alphabetical order.

The **musical alphabet** stops at G, then returns to A.

On the staff, there are 5 line notes:

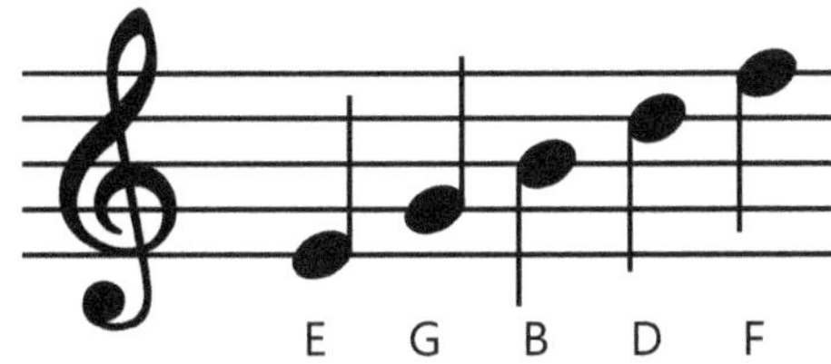


You can remember the names of the line notes by remembering this saying:
**E**very **G**ood **B**ird **D**oes **F**ly

On the staff, there are 4 line notes:

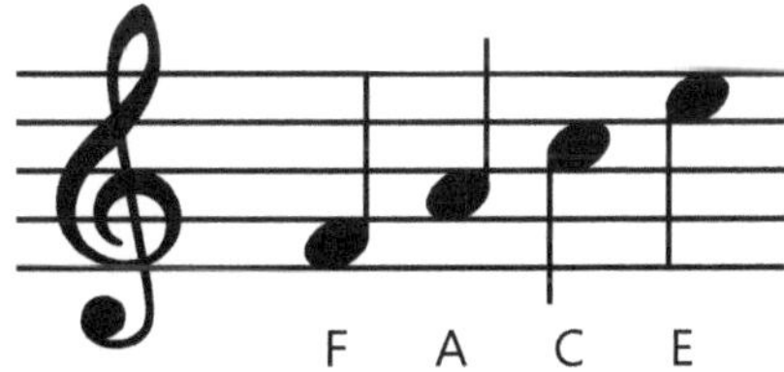


You can remember the names of space notes because they spell a word that rhymes with space = **F A C E**

Notice this symbol:  It's called a **treble clef**.

A **clef** is a symbol at the start of a piece of music that tells you how high or low the music on the staff is. A **treble clef** is used for high pitched instruments like the violin.

# Practice Naming and Drawing Notes

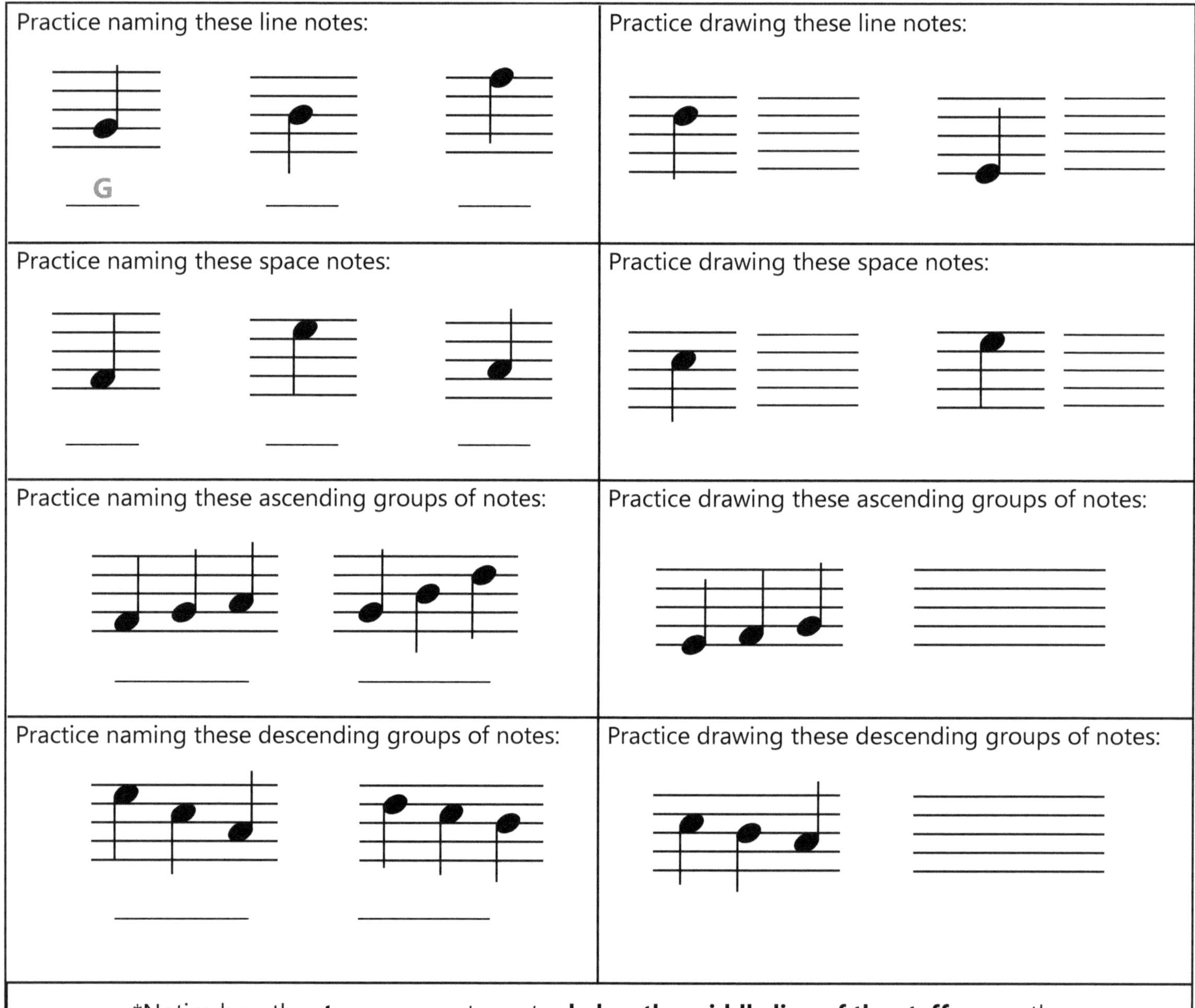


*Notice how the **stems** on quarter notes **below the middle line of the staff** are on the right side of the note, pointing up, and stems on quarter notes **on or above the middle line of the staff** are on the left side of the note, pointing down.

**Ascending**: moving up

Notice: when ascending notes step up one at a time, the note names are in alphabetical order.

**Descending**: moving down

Notice: when desceding notes step down one at a time, the note names are in reverse alphabetical order.

# Stepping and Skipping

The distance between 2 notes is called an **Interval.**

Notes can move up or down in **stepwise** motion:

**Notice this pattern!** When notes move in stepwise motion they alternate between line notes and space notes, and the note names move alphabetically (forwards or backwards).

And notes can move with **skips** between notes:

Notice how the line notes are skipped in the example above.

Skips can be small or large.

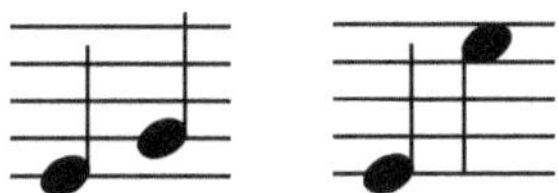

**How steps work on the violin**

When you add one finger at a time on a single string (0 1 2 3 4) the notes will move up in stepwise motion and alphabetical order.

For example on the A string, 0 fingers is A, 1 finger is B, 2 fingers is C, 3 fingers is D and 4 fingers is E.

Step or Skip?

Draw these notes, then name them and label as steps or skips

draw:

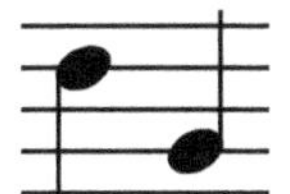

draw:

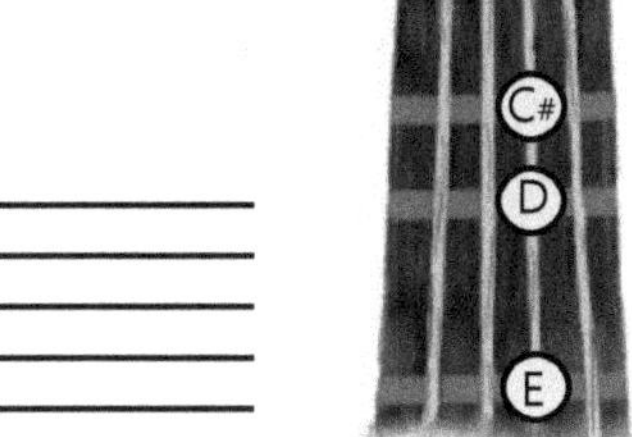


notes: ___ ___ step or skip? _______ notes: ___ ___ step or skip? _______

# How the Violin Works

The violin has 4 strings, tuned to specific notes. These notes are, from lowest to highest, G, D, A and E.

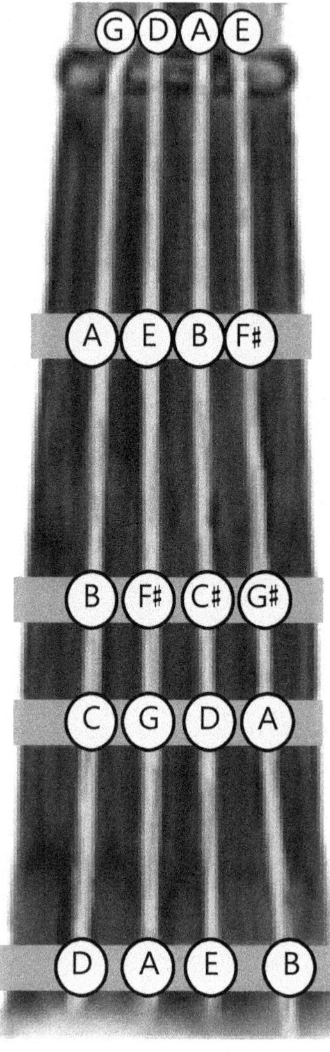


Write a saying to help you remember the order of the strings G D A E
Example: Good Dogs Are Everywhere

______________________________

When a string is played without any fingers, it's called an **open string.**

This symbol ♯ is called a sharp.
Sharps are explained on page 34.

There should be 3-4 finger tapes on the violin, which show where the fingers are placed on the strings to produce different pitches.

Notice how the thumb doesn't have a number because it isn't used to play notes on the fingerboard.

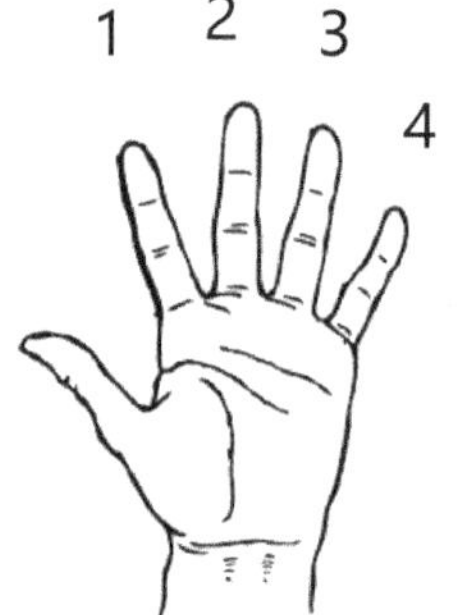


Reading the note names from the violin pictured, can you follow the musical alphabet all the way from 1 on G to 3 on E?
Both notes are named A, but the A on the G string will sound much lower than the A on the E string.

Notice how there are multiple As, Bs, Cs etc. on the violin. The distance between the A on the G string and open A is called an **octave.**

**Grab your violin!**
Silently tap your first, second, third and fourth fingers on each string saying the note name for each finger as you tap. If the note is written as F♯, say "F sharp".

example: Tap your first finger on the first finger tape on the D string and say "E".

Notice how the name of each 4th finger is the same as the open string above.

# Violin Notes on the Staff

Here are the notes we've learned so far

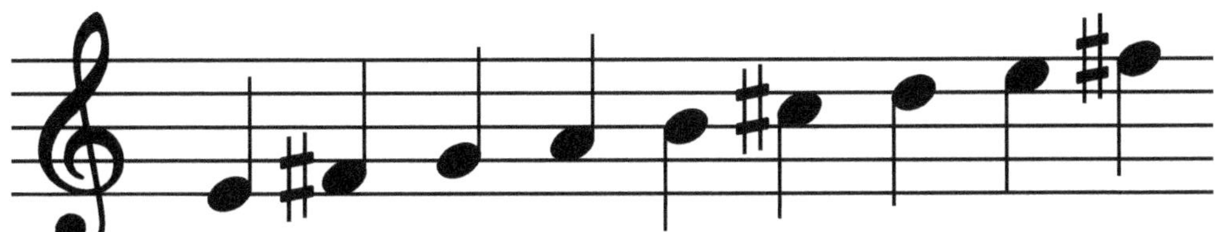

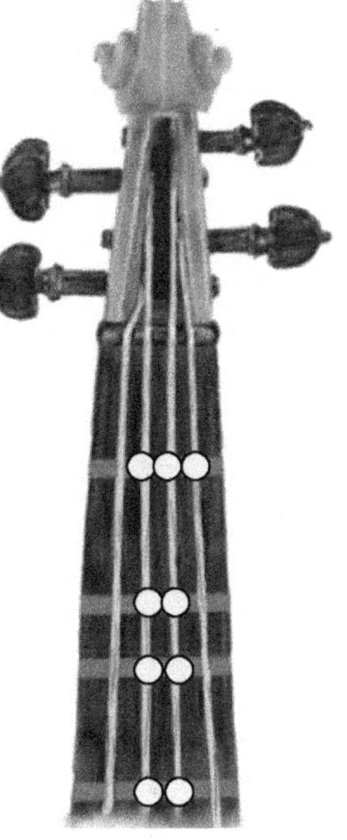

And where they're played on the violin:

Notice how there are a lot of notes on the violin that are higher or lower than the 9 notes that fit on the staff.

These notes are written using **ledger lines**: extra lines drawn above or below the staff

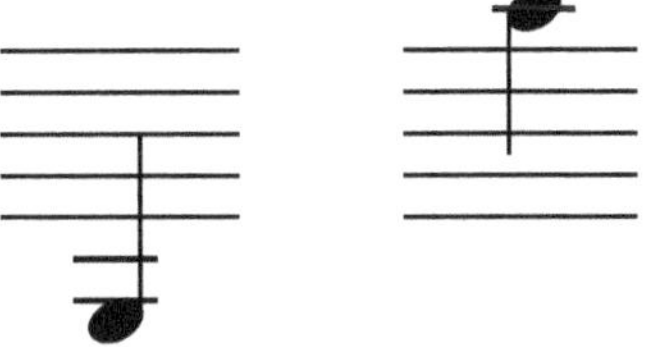

Here are all the notes on the violin, from open G to 4th finger on E, with open strings in bold

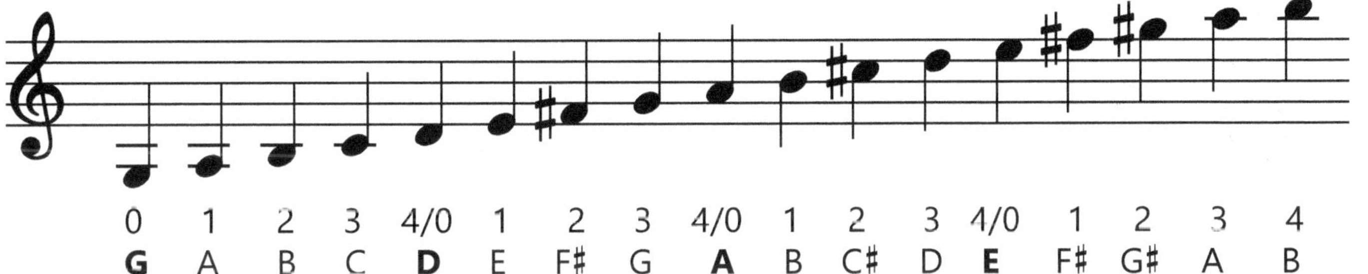


**Grab your violin!**

With your violin, try playing these notes by starting on open G and adding 1 finger at a time (1 2 and 3), then moving on to the open D string, play 1 2 3, then open A, 1 2 3, and finally open E, 1 2 3 and 4.

**4th finger:**

Notice how 4th finger or open strings can be used to play D, A and E, but open G can only be open because it's the lowest string, and B on the E string can only be played with 4th finger because E is the highest string.

**Challenge**: Grab a stopwatch! How fast can you say the alphabet, A - G? Then, how fast can you say it backwards, G - A?

# Memorizing Open String Notes

Here's what the open strings look like on their own:

G:  D:  A:  E: 

Memorize the location of open string notes on the staff first, so you can find any fingered note by counting up from the nearest open string!

Example: if this is open A... 

...and this note is one note higher than open A... 

... then it is played using **first finger** on the A string

**Practice drawing**

Open G: add 2 ledger lines below the staff, then draw G below the bottom line

  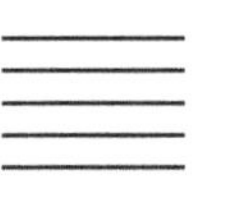 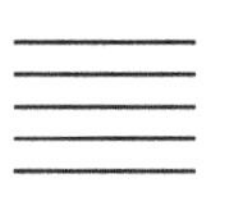 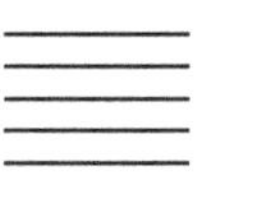 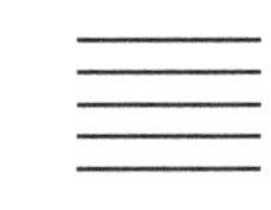

Open D: Draw D below the lowest line of the staff

  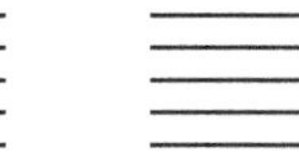 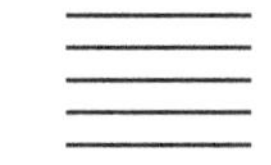 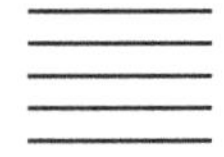

Open A: Draw A on the 2nd space of the staff

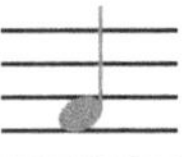 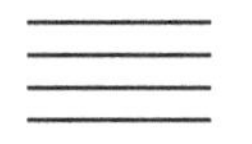 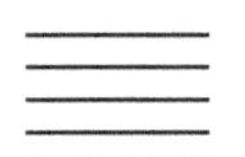 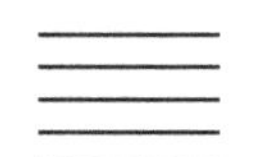 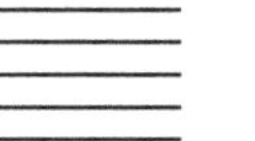 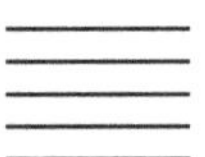

Open E: Draw E on the top space of the staff

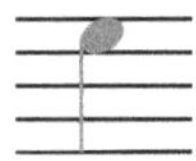 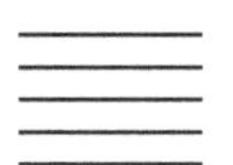 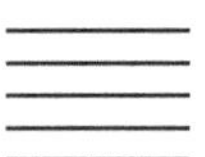 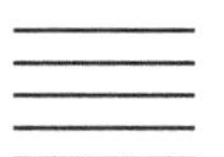 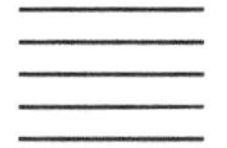 

**Open string? Yes or No**

_____ _____ _____ _____ _____ _____

# Notes on the A string

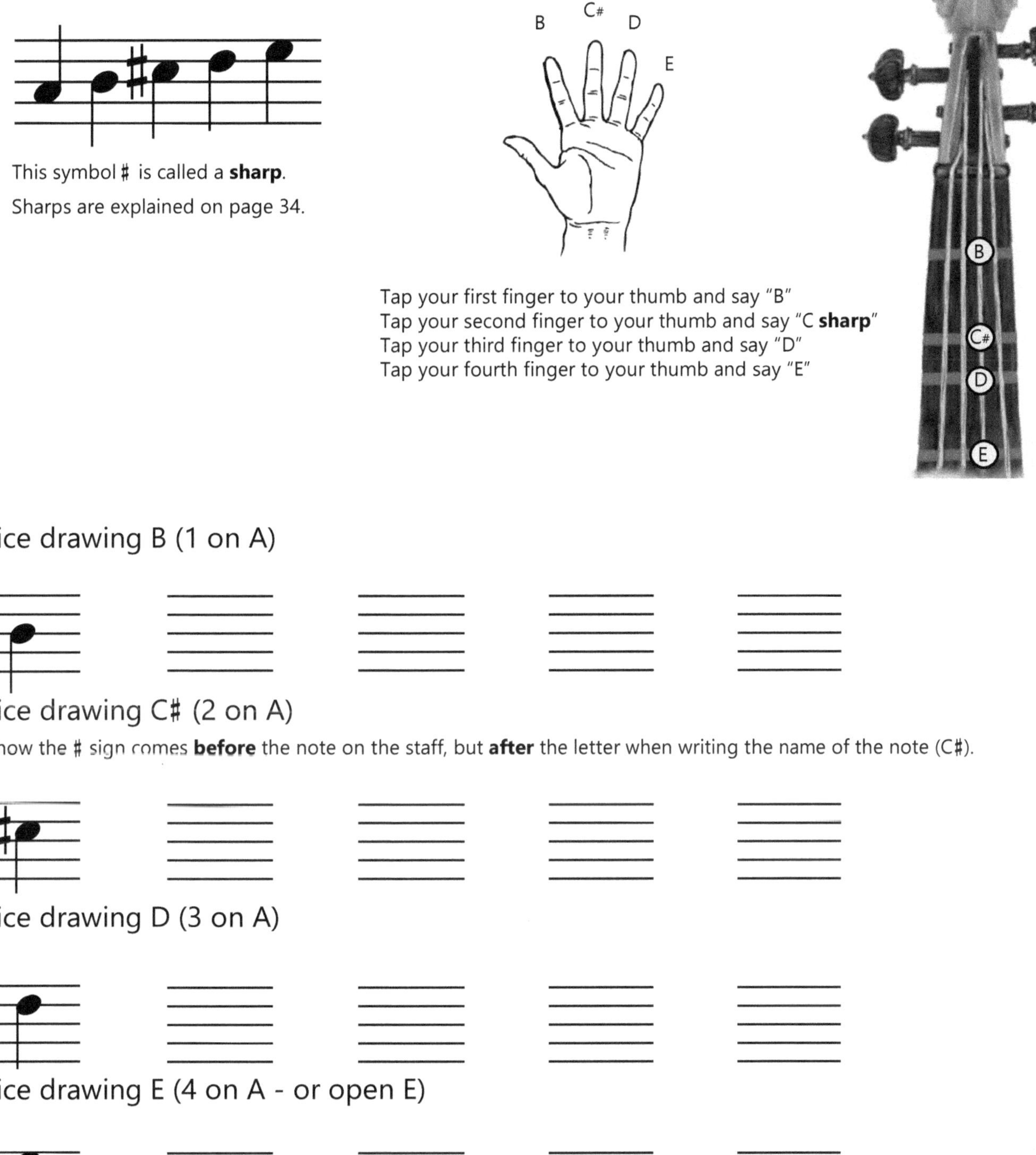


This symbol ♯ is called a **sharp**.
Sharps are explained on page 34.

Tap your first finger to your thumb and say "B"
Tap your second finger to your thumb and say "C **sharp**"
Tap your third finger to your thumb and say "D"
Tap your fourth finger to your thumb and say "E"

## Practice drawing B (1 on A)

## Practice drawing C♯ (2 on A)

Notice how the ♯ sign comes **before** the note on the staff, but **after** the letter when writing the name of the note (C♯).

## Practice drawing D (3 on A)

## Practice drawing E (4 on A - or open E)

# A string Quiz

Are these notes on the A string? Yes or No

How do you play these notes on the A string (write the finger number)

Write the letter and finger number for each note

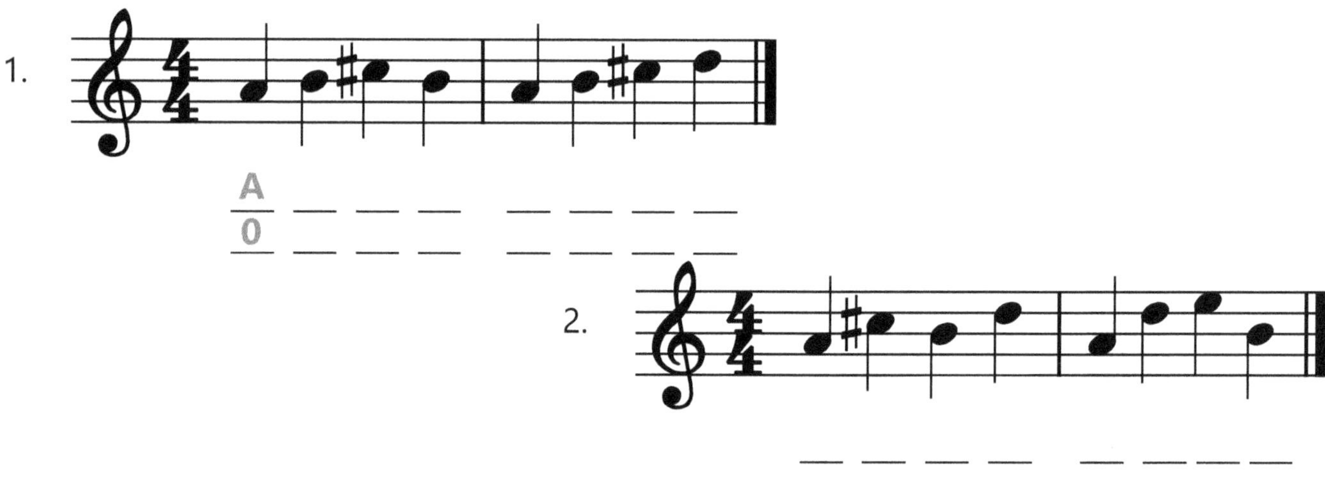


Can you play these notes on the violin?

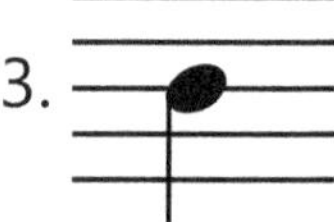

# Notes on the D string

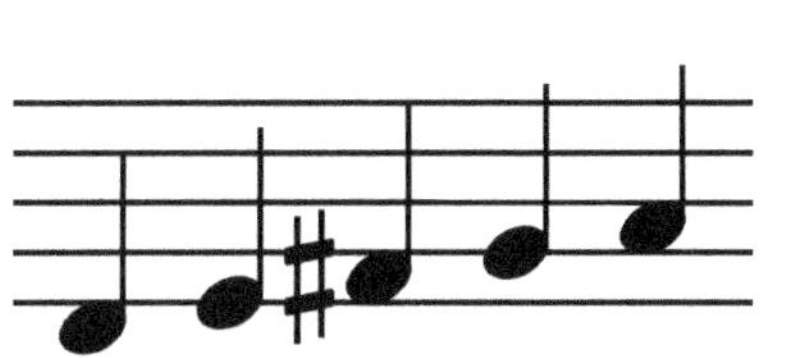

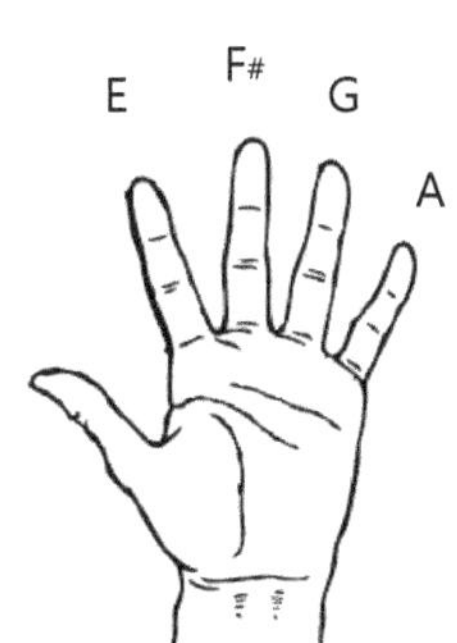


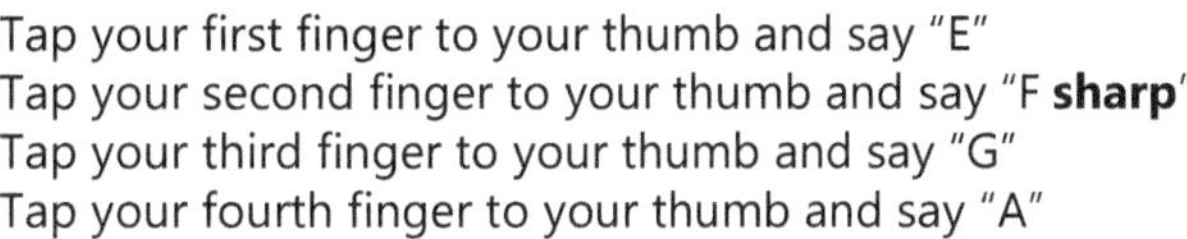


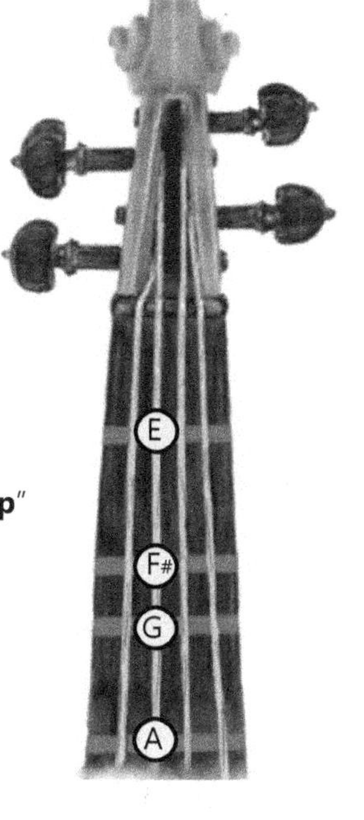


Practice drawing E (1 on D)

Practice drawing F♯(2 on D)

Practice drawing G (3 on D)

Practice drawing A (4 on D - or open A)

# D string Quiz

Are these notes on the D string? Yes or No

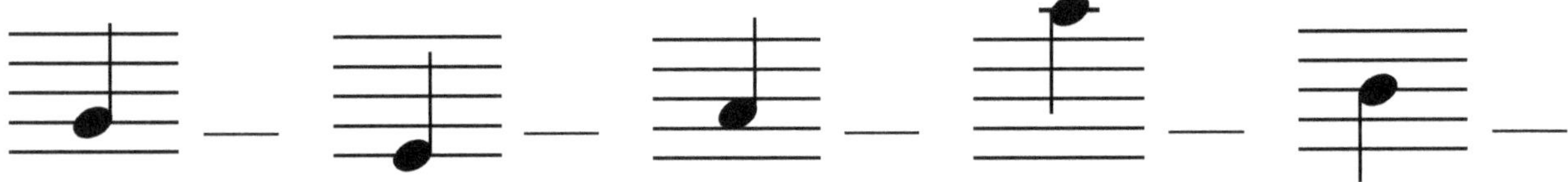

How do you play these notes on the D string (write the finger number)

Write the letter and finger number for each note

Can you play these notes on the violin?

1. 

2. 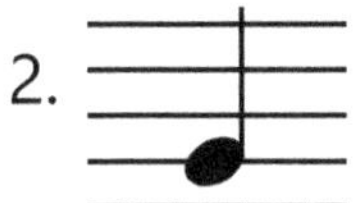

3. 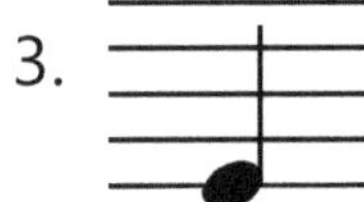

4. 

5. 

6. 

7. 

# Notes on the E string

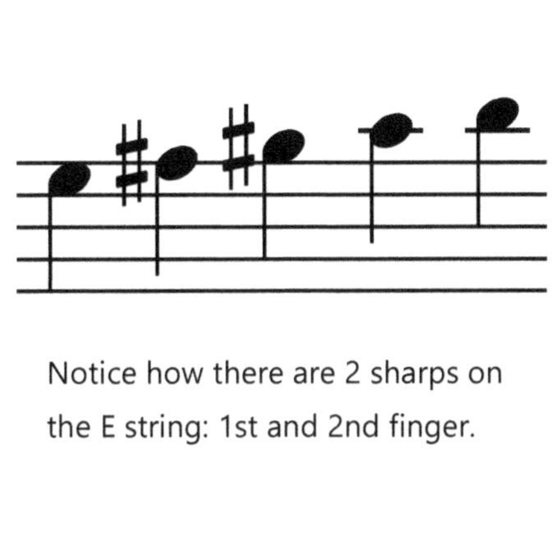

Notice how there are 2 sharps on the E string: 1st and 2nd finger.

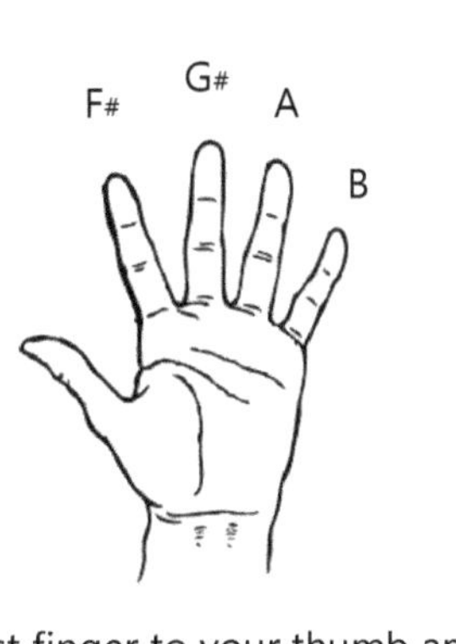


Tap your first finger to your thumb and say "F **sharp**"
Tap your second finger to your thumb and say "G **sharp**"
Tap your third finger to your thumb and say "A"
Tap your fourth finger to your thumb and say "B"

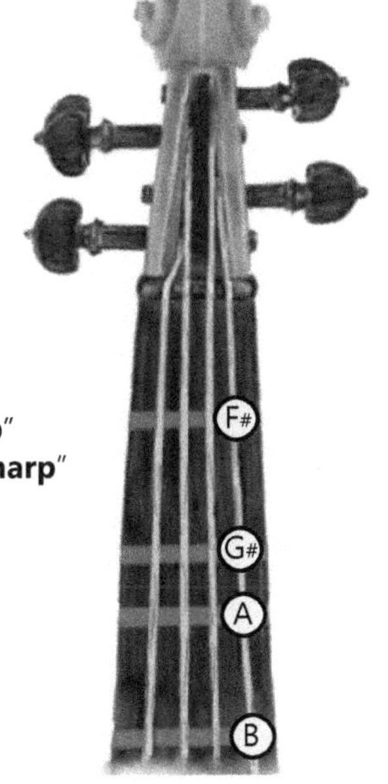


Practice drawing F♯ (1 on E)

Practice drawing G♯ (2 on E)

Practice drawing A (3 on E)

Practice drawing B (4 on E)

# E string Quiz

Are these notes on the E string? Yes or No

How do you play these notes on the E string (write the finger number)

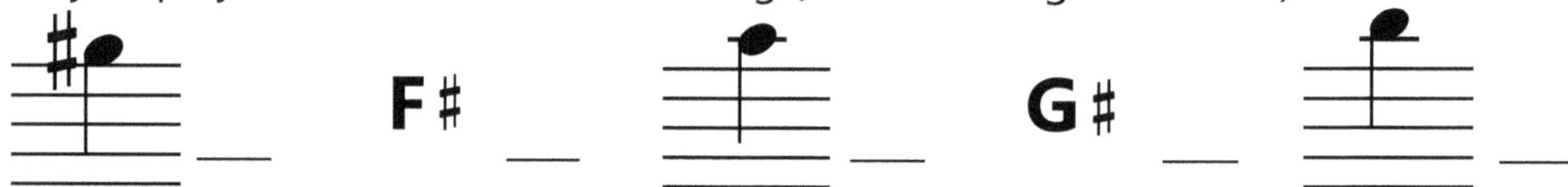


Write the letter and finger number for each note

1.

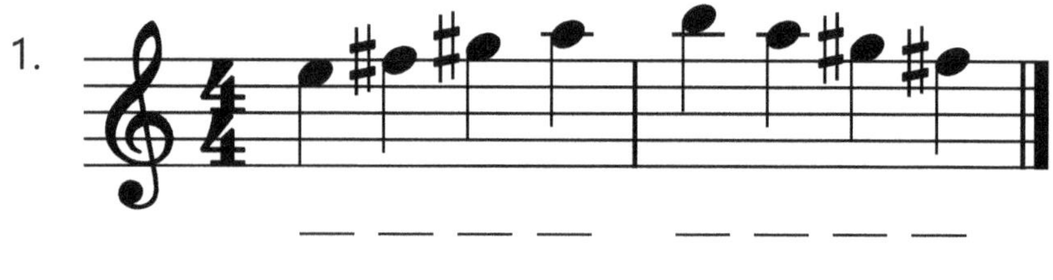

2.

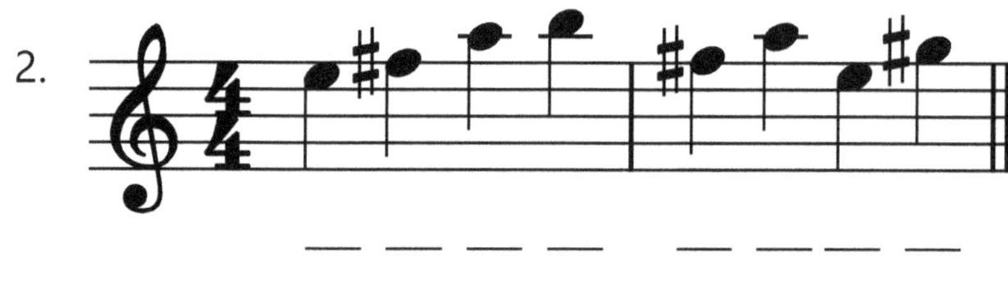

Can you play these notes on the violin?

1.

2.

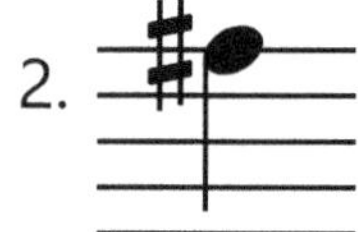

3.

4.

5.

6.

7.

# Notes on the G string

Notice how there are no sharps on the G string

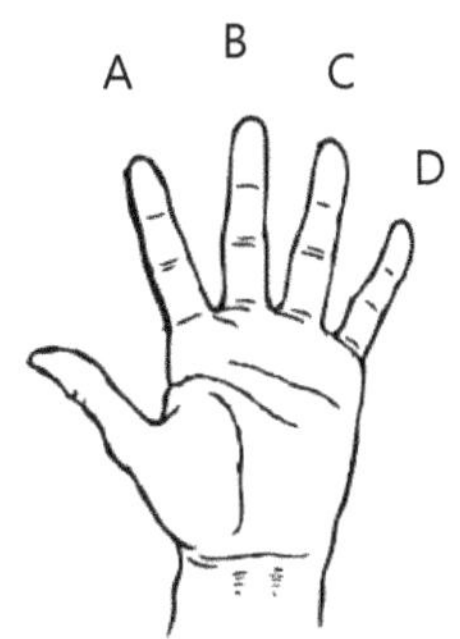


Tap your first finger to your thumb and say "A"
Tap your second finger to your thumb and say "B"
Tap your third finger to your thumb and say "C"
Tap your fourth finger to your thumb and say "D"

Practice drawing A (1 on G)

Practice drawing B (2 on G)

Practice drawing C (3 on G)

Practice drawing D (4 on G - or open D)

# G string Quiz

Are these notes on the G string? Yes or No

How do you play these notes on the G string (write the finger number)

Write the letter and finger number for each note

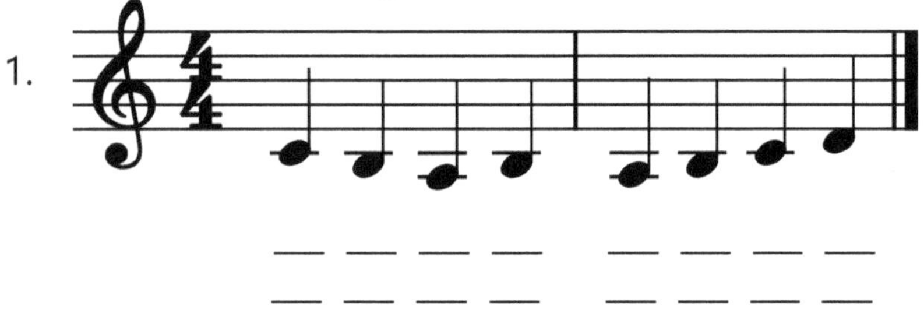


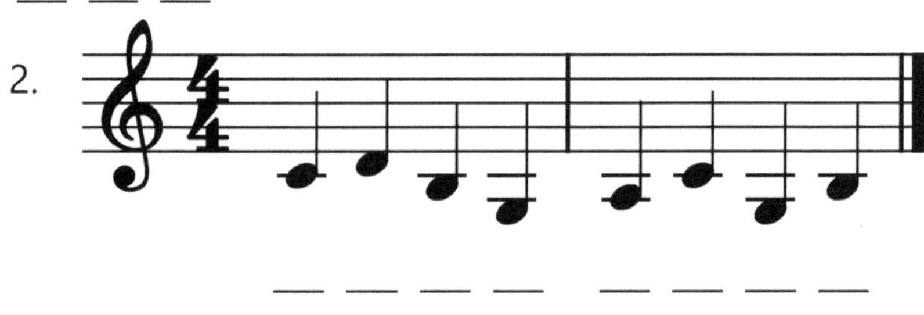


Can you play these notes on the violin?

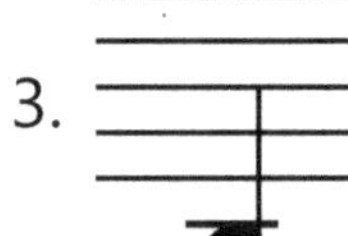

# Say and Play Open String Scales

A **scale** is a set of notes that go up or down one step at a time.

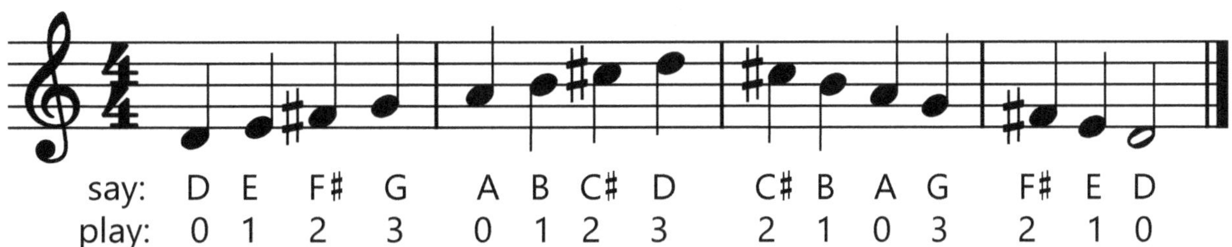


**Scales are named after the note they start and end on.**
The D major scale shown above starts on open D and steps up, alphabetically, to the next D (3 on A) before turning around and stepping back down to open D.

The following scales all start on open strings. Play each scale on the violin while saying the note names out loud.

D major scale

A major scale

G major scale

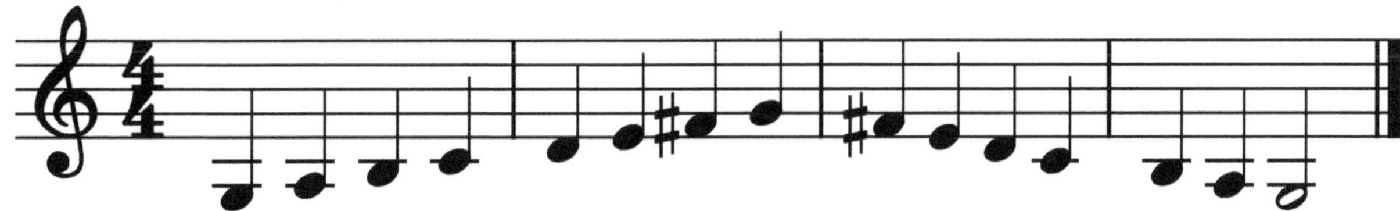

**Challenge**:
Grab a stopwatch! See how long it takes to say and play the scale. If you're able to go up and down a scale quickly without pausing, saying the correct note names for each finger, it's a sign the note names are becoming second nature.

# Note Name Review

Write the note name for each finger tape. Remember to include sharps (♯)s!

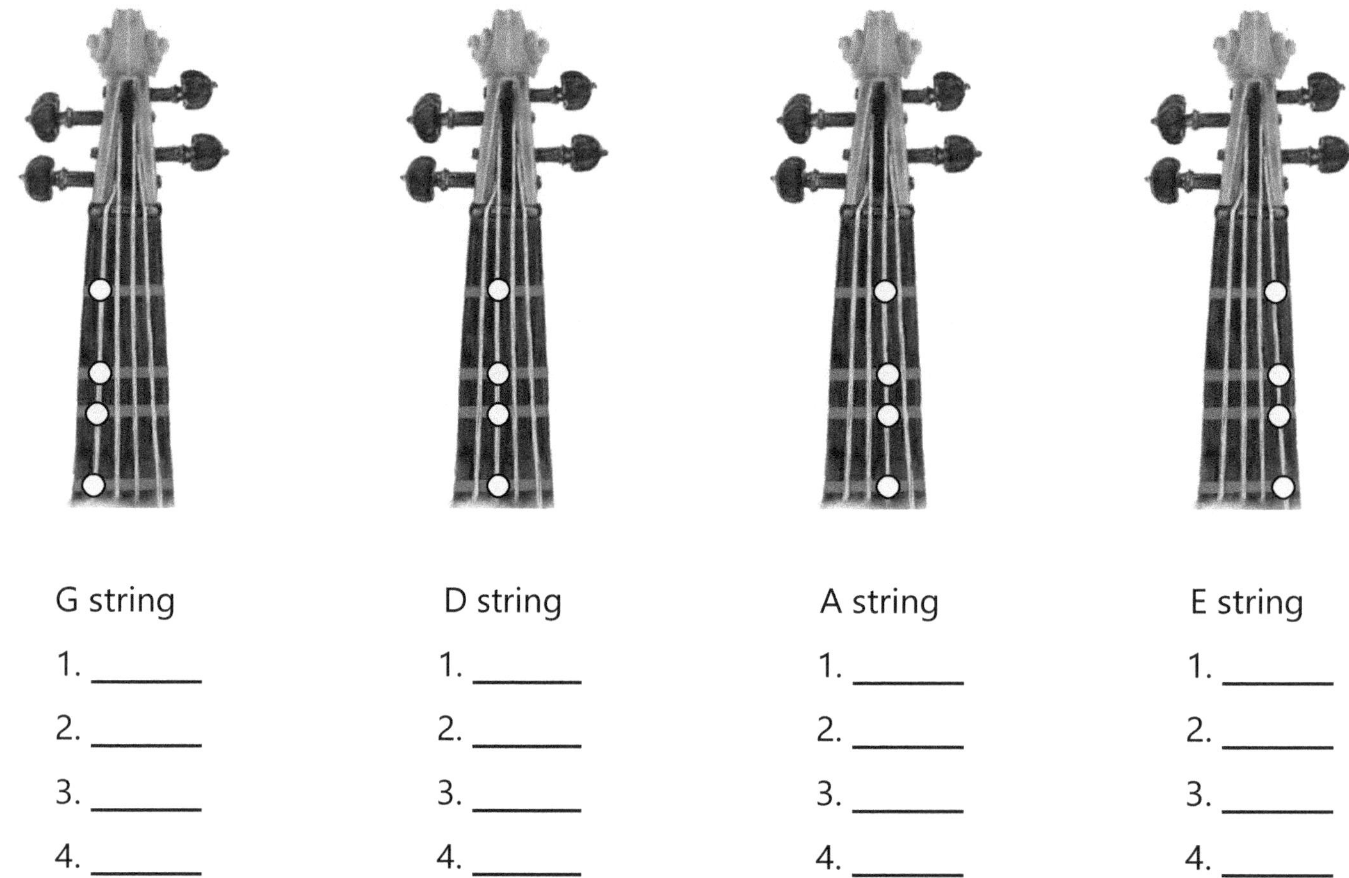


Draw a scale on the staff using quarter notes that starts on open G and ends on G on the D string. Label each note using finger numbers and note names - don't forget to add the sharps both by the note on the staff and when you label the note name.

__ __ __ __   __ __ __ __   __ __ __ __   __ __ __

__ __ __ __   __ __ __ __   __ __ __ __   __ __ __

# Vocabulary lesson

**Treble Clef**: A symbol at the start of a piece of music that tells you how high or low the music on the staff is.

**Key Signature**: Appears at the beginning of a piece of music to show what notes are sharp or flat in the piece.

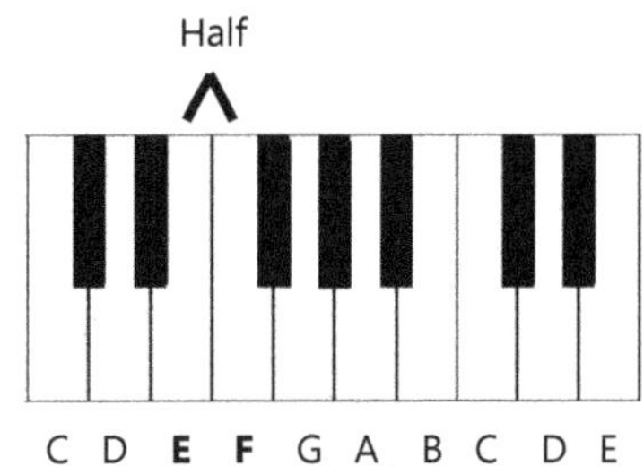


**Half step**: The distance between two notes that are right next to each other on a piano keyboard. In this book, half steps are labeled using this symbol: ʌ

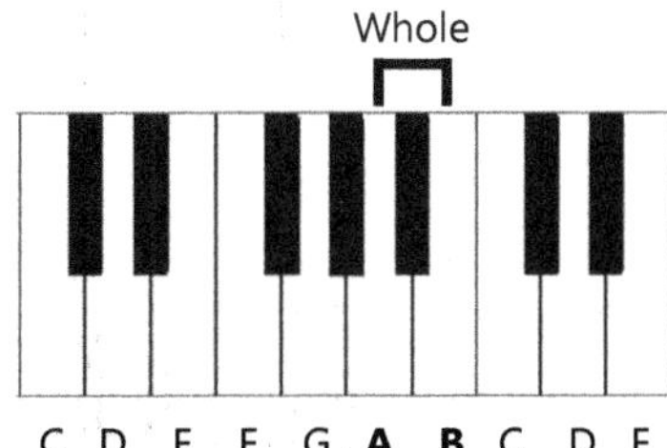


**Whole step**: The distance between two notes that have step-wise letter names (ex. A and B) but have two half steps between them. In this book, whole steps are labeled using this symbol: ⊓

♯ **Sharp**: A sharp raises a natural note by a half step.

♭ **Flat**: A flat lowers a natural note by a half step.

♮ **Natural**: A note that is not sharp or flat is called a natural note. All of the white keys on a piano keyboard are "natural" notes. To avoid filling the staff with symbols, assume notes are natural unless the key signature labels them sharp or flat, or a sharp or flat appears in the music before the note.

# Why are some of the finger tape notes #?

In the musical alphabet, there are 7 different note names: A B C D E F G
**However**, Western music uses 12 different notes - take a look at this piano keyboard and count all the keys (white and black) from C to B.

A B **C D E F G A B** C D E

On a piano keyboard, the white keys are the 7 natural notes.
The black keys are the notes in between the natural notes - the sharps and flats.

A **sharp** ♯ raises a natural note by a half step,
so the black key above C is used to play C♯.

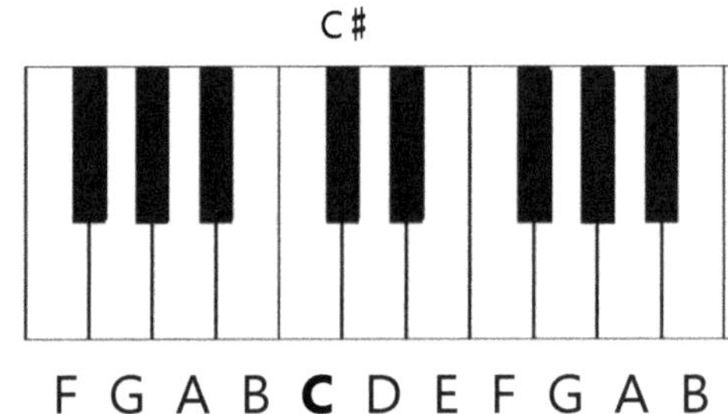


F G A B **C** D E F G A B

A **flat** ♭ lowers a natural note by a half step,
so the black key below D is used to play D♭.

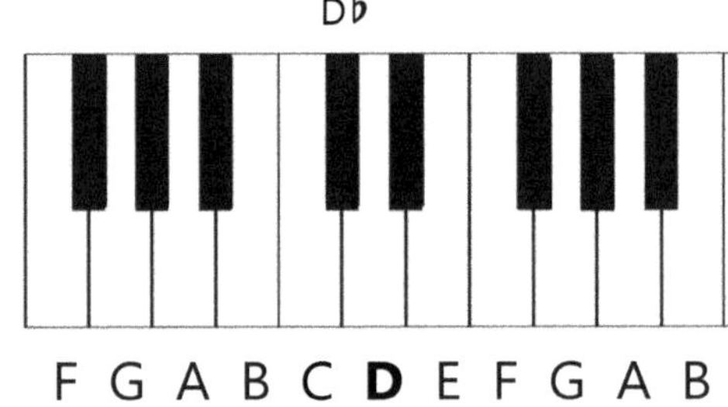


F G A B C **D** E F G A B

Notice how C sharp and D flat are played using the same black key!
C♯ and D♭ are **enharmonic equivalents** - two notes that sound the same, but are labeled differently depending on the key signature of a piece.

Notice how there are **no black keys between B and C and between E and F**.
The distance between most natural notes is a whole step (skips a black key), but the distance between these two sets of notes is a half step.

# Half and Whole Steps on the Violin

Here is a piano keyboard with all the notes labeled:

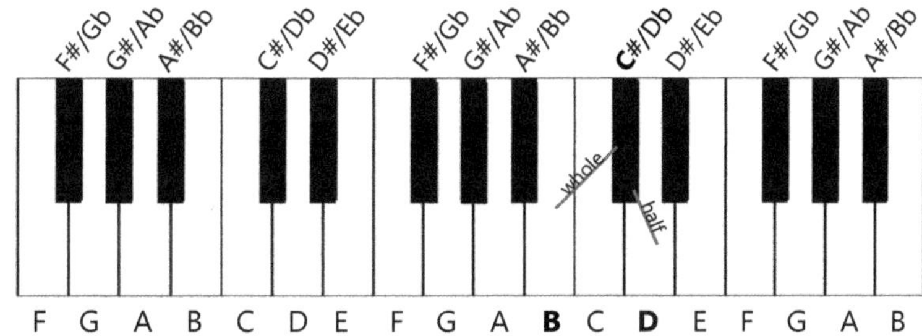


A half step is the distance between 2 notes that are right next to each other, like C♯ and D
A whole step skips over one note, like B to C♯ (skips over C).

Now take a look at the fingertapes on the violin: notice how the tapes aren't spaced evenly? The 2nd and 3rd fingertapes are closer together than the 1st and 2nd or the 3rd and 4th.

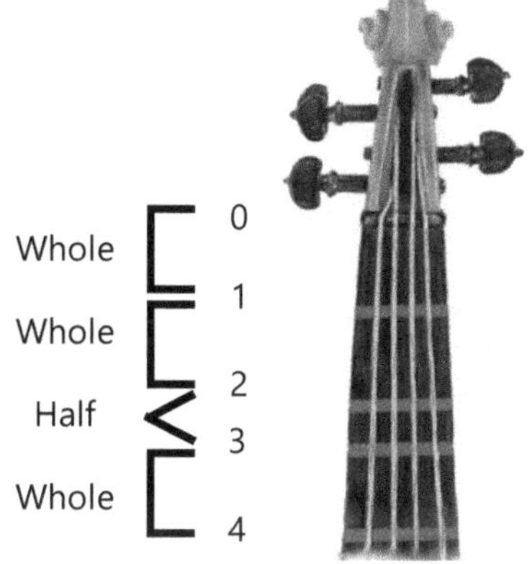


The distance between the first and second finger tape is a whole step.
The distance between the second and third finger tape is a half step.
The distance between the third and fourth finger tape is a whole step.

*The distance between an open string and the first finger tape is also a whole step.

**Comparing Violin and Piano**

Remember the names of the notes on the 2nd and 3rd finger tapes. Find each pair of notes on the piano keyboard (B-C, F♯-G, C♯-D and G♯-A). Notice how they're all half steps.

Now compare the 1st and 2nd finger notes on the violin with the notes on the piano (A-B, E-F♯, B-C♯, F♯-G♯). Notice how they're all whole steps.

# Explaining Low 2

Q: If the 2nd finger tape on the A string is used to play C sharp, how do you play C natural?

A: C natural is played by placing the 2nd finger between the 1st and 2nd finger tapes: this is called a **low 2**

Note: On the page, it looks like low 2 is located above the 2nd finger tape. It's called a low 2 because
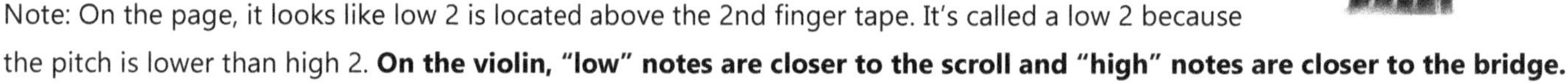
the pitch is lower than high 2. **On the violin, "low" notes are closer to the scroll and "high" notes are closer to the bridge.**

Compare the notes on the A string (including low 2) to their location on a piano keyboard. Notice where the half steps and whole steps are on both instruments.

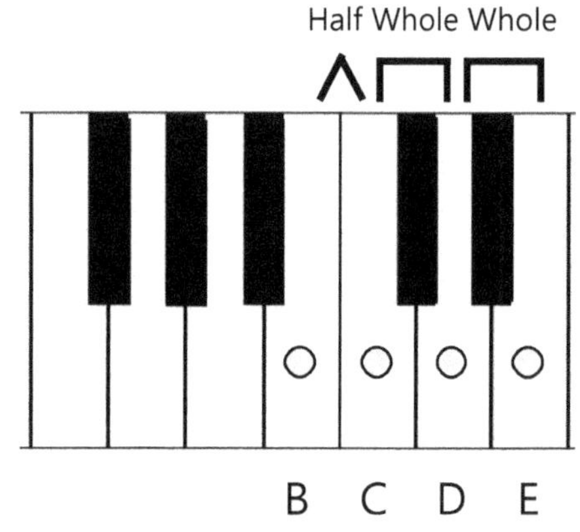


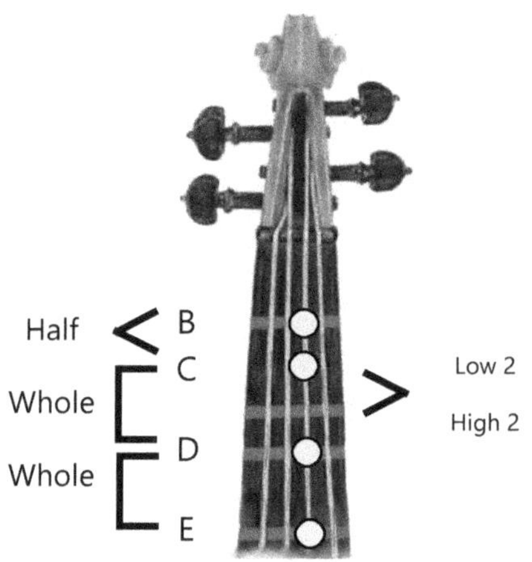


Low 2 is a half step lower than 2 on the tape (we'll call the "tape 2" "high 2" from now on) What is the name of the note played by low 2 on each string?

| A string: | E string: |
|---|---|
| High 2: C sharp | High 2: ____________ |
| Low 2: C natural | Low 2: ____________ |
| | |
| D string: | G string: |
| High 2: ____________ | High 2: ____________ |
| Low 2: ____________ | Low 2: ____________ |

# High and Low Fingers

Including low 2nd finger notes, here are all of the notes we know how to play on the violin so far:

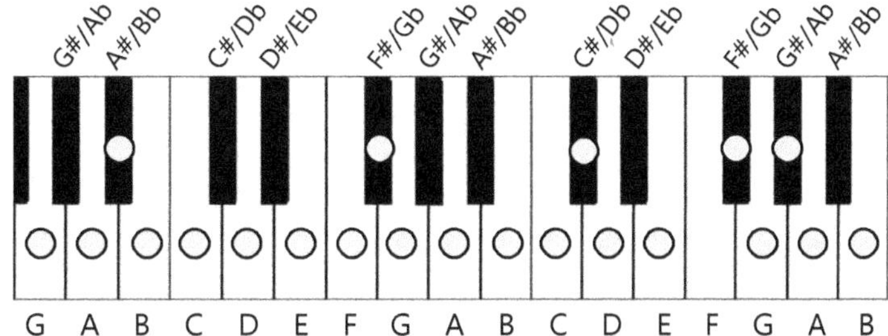


All of the remaining notes can be played by raising or lowering 1st, 3rd or 4th fingers

Notice how High 3 and Low 4 are the same place on the violin, and each black key on the piano has 2 note name options - one sharp and one flat. These notes are **enharmonic**, meaning they sound the same but they might be labeled either sharp or flat depending on the other notes surrounding them.

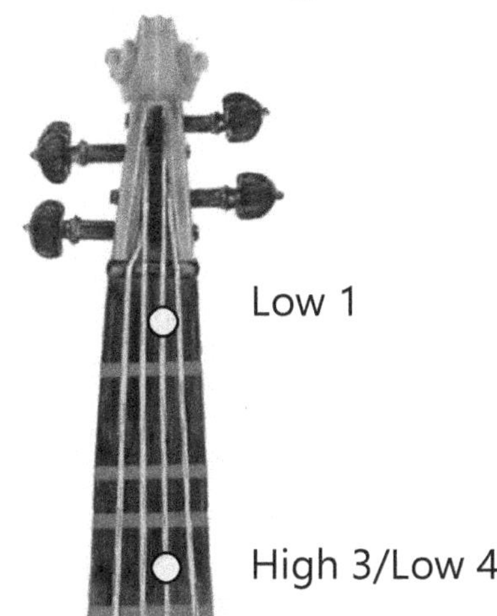


Take D♯/Eb for example. It could be played using high 3 or low 4 on the A string, and it could be written as D♯ or E♭ on the staff.

The Finger Name Rule:

* In general, it is helpful to **assign each finger a letter name for each string**. For example, on the A string, 1st finger is the B finger, 2nd finger is the C finger, 3rd finger is the D finger, and 4th finger is the E finger. This way, even though D♯ and E♭ are the same note, D♯ would be played using high 3rd finger, and E♭ would be played using low 4th finger.

D♭ would be played using 3rd finger as well - and because D♭ is the same note as C♯, D♭ is played by placing 3rd finger on the 2nd finger tape.

**One exception** of this rule might be in the case of low 1 verses high 4.

For example: 

The note above is a D sharp, and it could be played using a high 4th finger on the G string (a half step above 4 on G) or low 1 on D (a half step above open D). Even though 1st finger would usually be in charge of E notes on the D string, it might be easier to use low 1 to play D sharp instead of stretching 4th finger higher than the 4th finger tape.

# Every Note on the Violin

Below is a chart with the location of every note on the violin, from open G to 4th finger on E:

Name this Note:

If it looks like there are two letter options, remember the finger name rule from the previous page.

Low 2 on A: _______

High 3 on D: _______

Low 2 on E: _______

Low 1 on G: _______

Low 4 on D: _______

High 3 on A: _______

High 2 on G: _______

Low 1 on E: _______

How would you play this note?

D♯ on D: _______________

A♭ on G: _______________

B♭ on E: _______________

C♯ on A: _______________

E♭ on D: _______________

D♭ on A: _______________

C♯ on G: _______________

A♯ on E: _______________

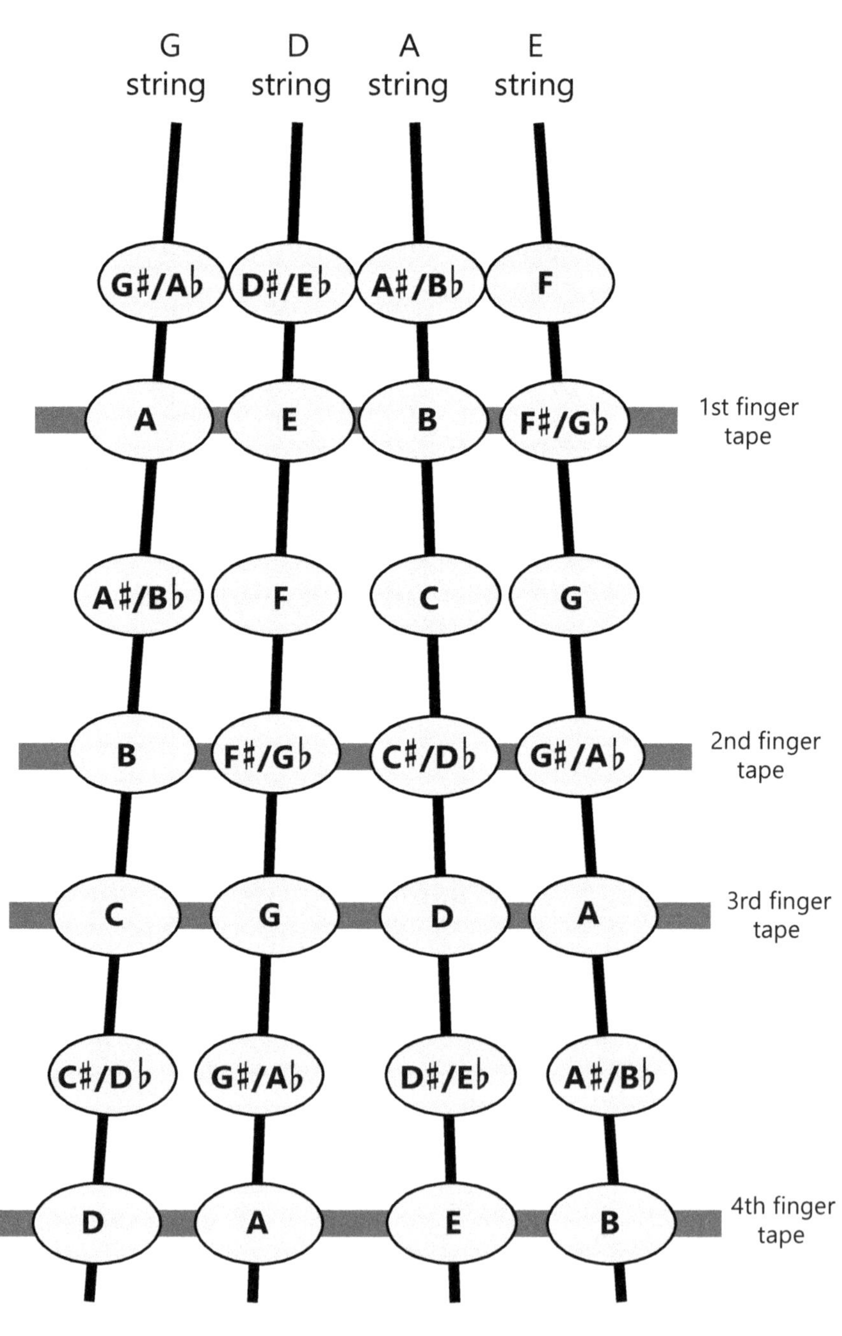

# Half Steps and Whole Steps Quiz

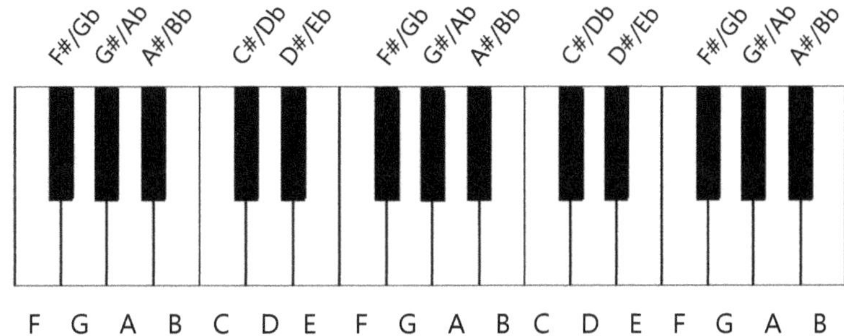


**Using the piano keyboard pictured above, answer the following questions:**

| | |
|---|---|
| 1. What note is a half step above C♯ ______ | 5. What note is a half step above G ______ |
| 2. What note is a whole step below B ______ | 6. What note is a whole step below A ______ |
| 3. What note is a half step below F ______ | 7. What note is a half step below E♭ ______ |
| 4. What note is a whole step above D ______ | 8. What note is a whole step above B ______ |

**Using the violin, answer the following questions:**

Whole or Half step?

1. A to B ________
2. C♯ to D ________
3. G to A ________
4. E to F ________
5. B♭ to C ________
6. F♯ to G ________

Which note is a half step above:

1. A ______
2. C ______
3. E ______
4. D ______
5. G♯ ______
6. B♭ ______

# Additional Practice

**How do you play this note?**

For each note on the staff below, draw a circle on the violin strings provided in the spot where you'd place your finger to play the note correctly.

If a note falls on a tape, label it with a finger number. If a note is not a "tape" note, label it "high" using "H", or "low" using "L". Example: high 3 = H3, low 2 = L2.

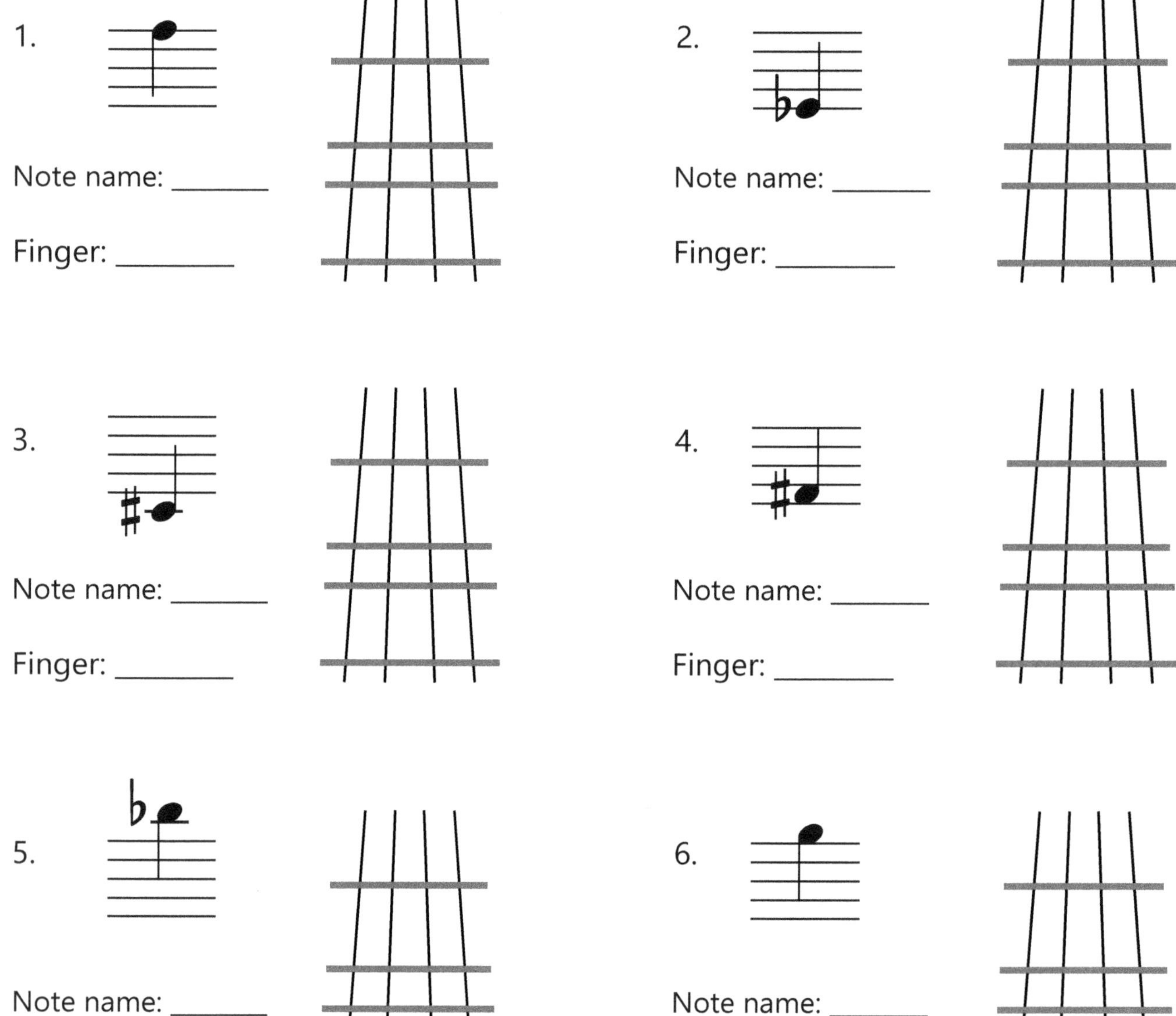

# How Many....?

For each natural note listed below, draw every possible location on the violin.
Draw open strings by placing a circle above the string (see example).

Example: G

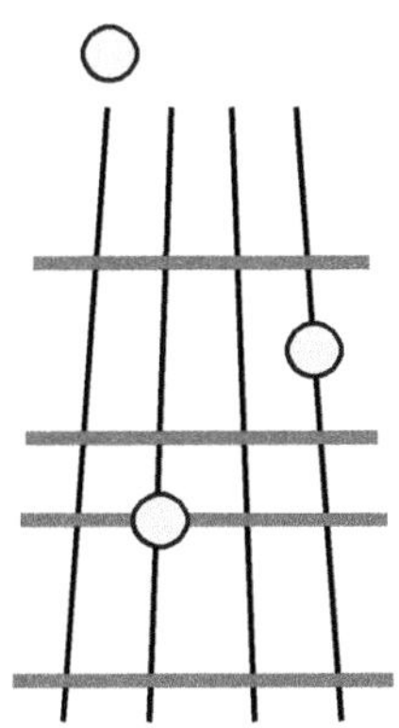

1. A

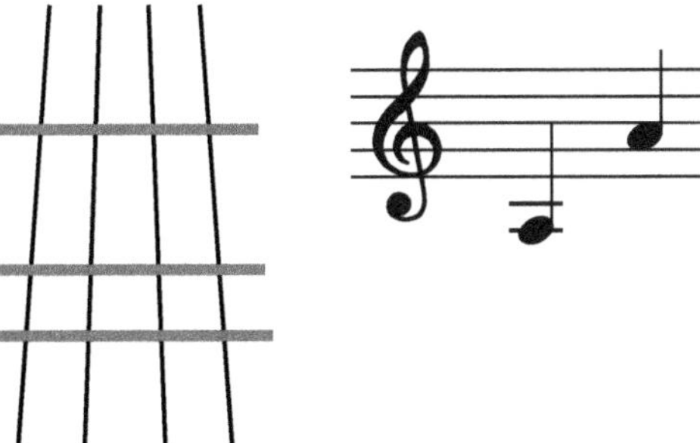

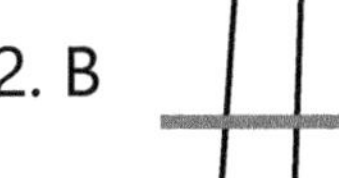

2. B

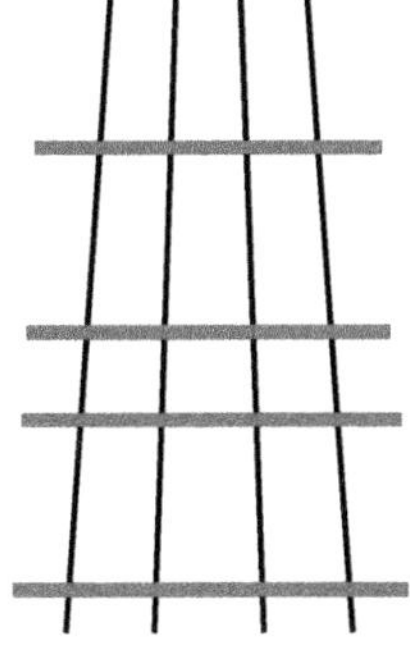

3. C

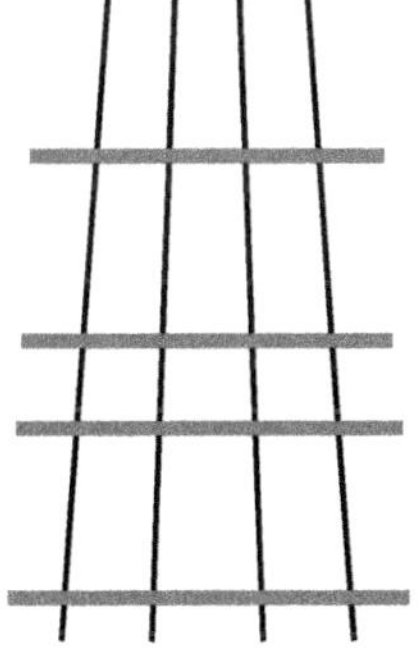

4. D

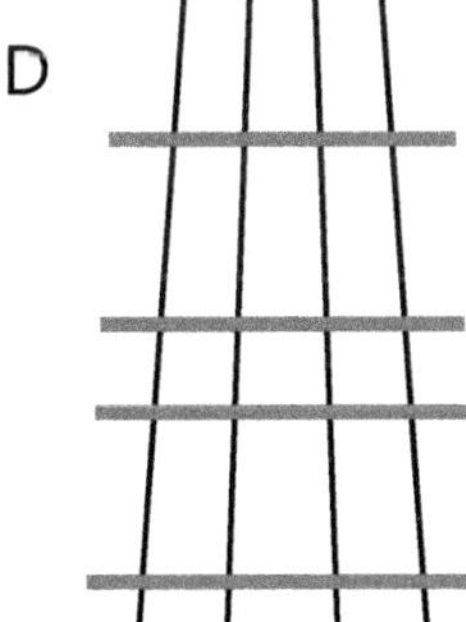

5. E

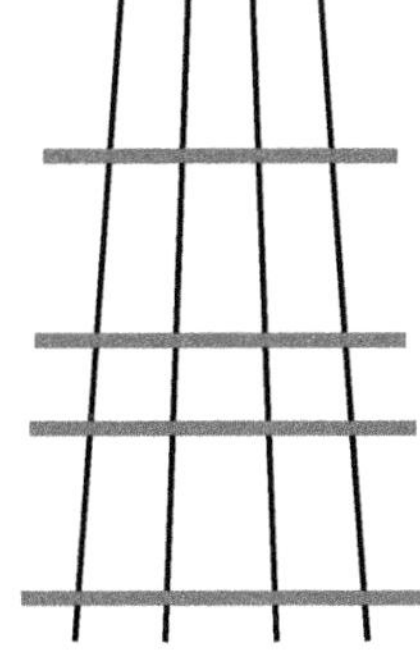

6. F

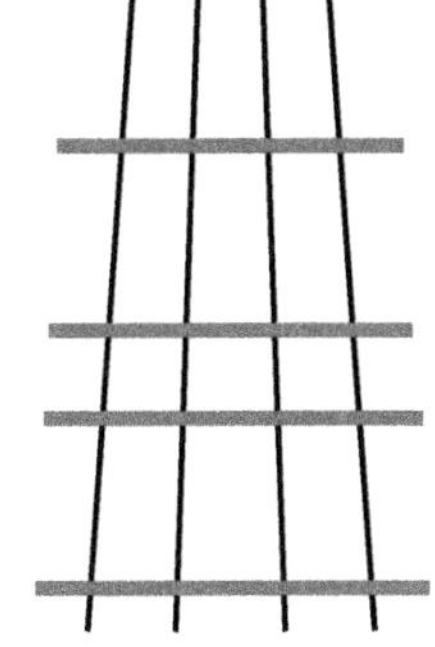

# Finger Pattern Practice

Write the names of the notes shown on each string, then draw them on the staff.

*Remember sharps and flats are written after the letter when you write or say the name (example C♯), and before the note when it's written on the staff:

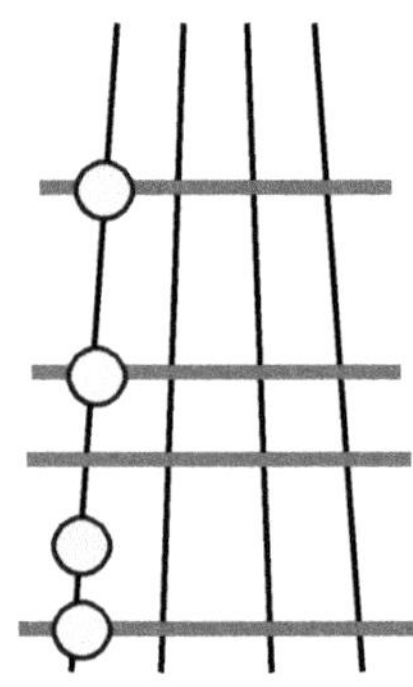

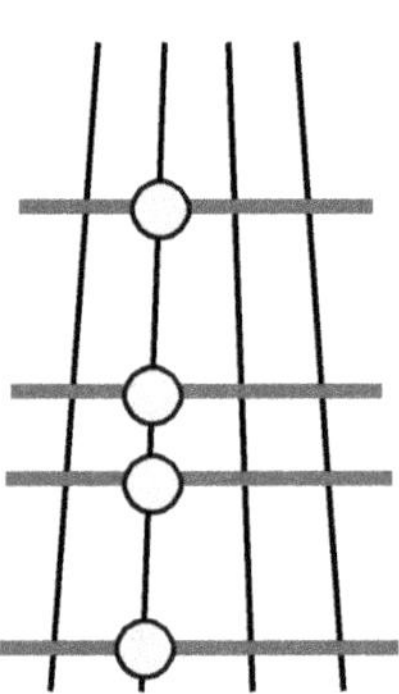

Note Names: ______________________

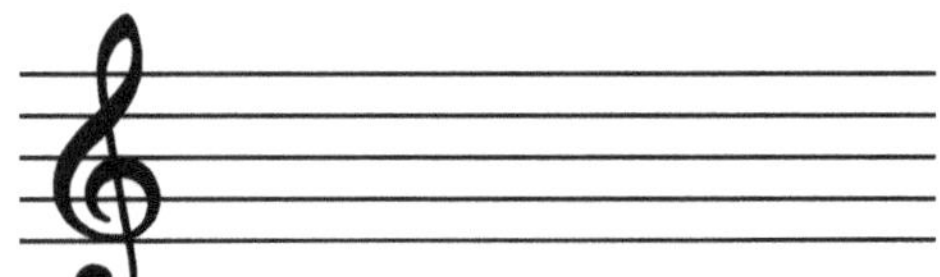

Note Names: ______________________

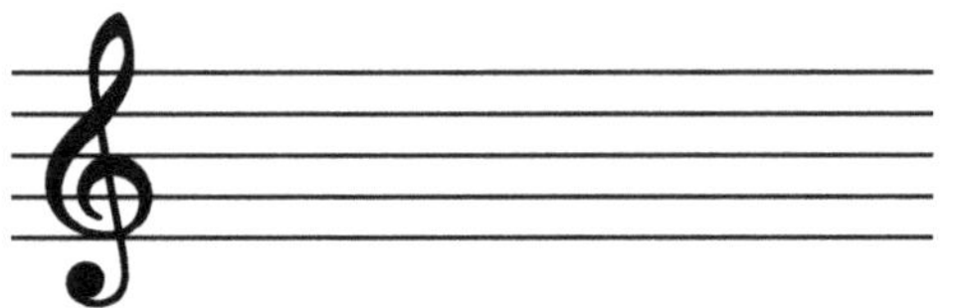

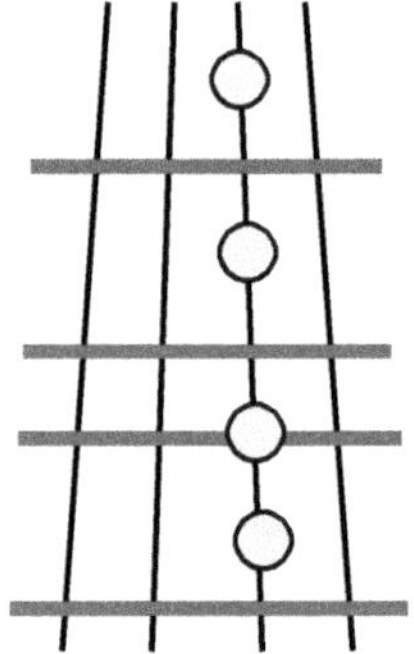

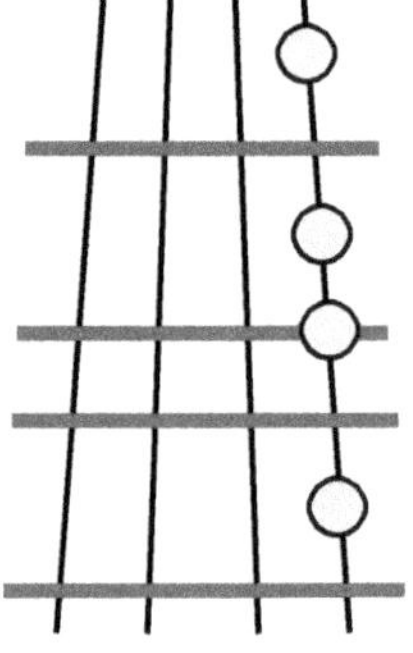

Note Names: ______________________

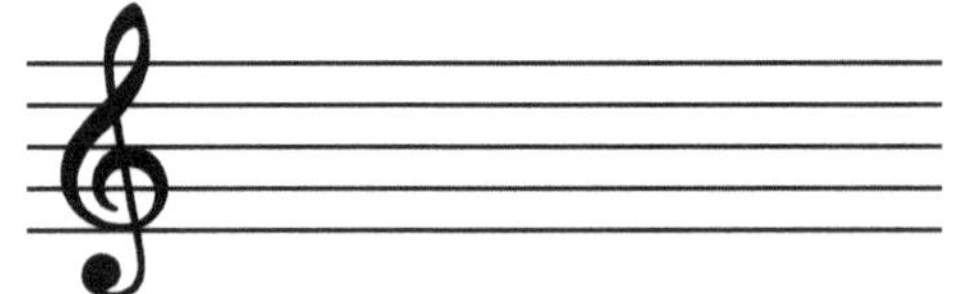

Note Names: ______________________

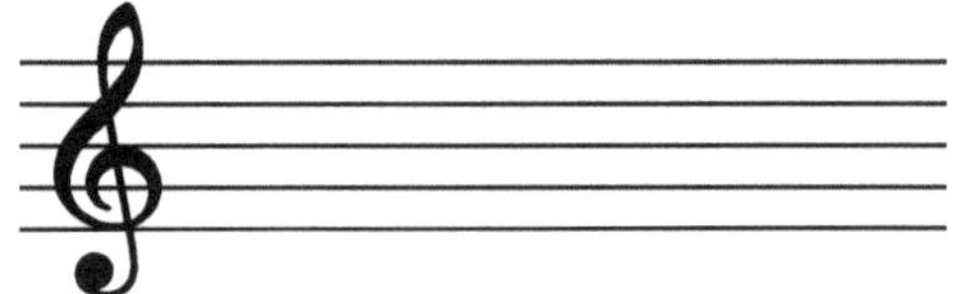

# Key signatures

Look back to page 31, Open String Scales.
Notice how in the A major scale, there were 3 sharp notes - F♯, G♯ and C♯.
Up to this point, sharps and flats have been labeled immediately before the notes on the staff.

However, labeling the notes in this way can make the music look cluttered. In the A major scale pictured above, F, C and G are always sharp. So rather than writing a sharp before every F, C and G, **a key signature can be placed at the beginning of the staff to symbolize that every F, C and G in the music will be sharp.**

Notice where the sharps appear on the staff for the key signature. If you were to draw notes on the same lines and spaces as the sharps appear, you'd get the notes F, C and G.

This means that every F, C and G in the music is sharp, **in any octave.** Therefore, even though the F♯ in the key signature is drawn on the E string location, the F on the D string will also be sharp.

When learning a new piece of music, it's important to check the key signature to know which notes will be sharp, flat and natural throughout the piece.

**Accidentals**

Even when key signatures are used, it's common to see additional sharps or flats on the staff in a piece of music.

These extra sharps, flats and naturals that don't belong in the key signature are called **accidentals**, and they alter the pitch of a note for the duration of one measure.

Accidentals are canceled by the bar line, so the sharp in the example above applies to both As in that measure, but the A in the following measure is natural again.

# Key Signature Practice

What notes are sharp in these key signatures?
(Hint: Draw noteheads in the same location as the sharps, then name the notes you've drawn to see which notes are sharp in the key signature)

Example:

answer F♯

1.

answer ________________

Do the same with these flat keys

2.

answer ________________

3.

answer ________________

What key signature fits these scales?
(Hint: first, label every note, remembering to include the sharps or flats. Circle the sharp/flat notes. Then, circle the key signature that includes all the flats or sharps in the scale).

Example:

Example:

# More Practice with Finger Patterns

Match these A string finger patterns to the correct key signature:

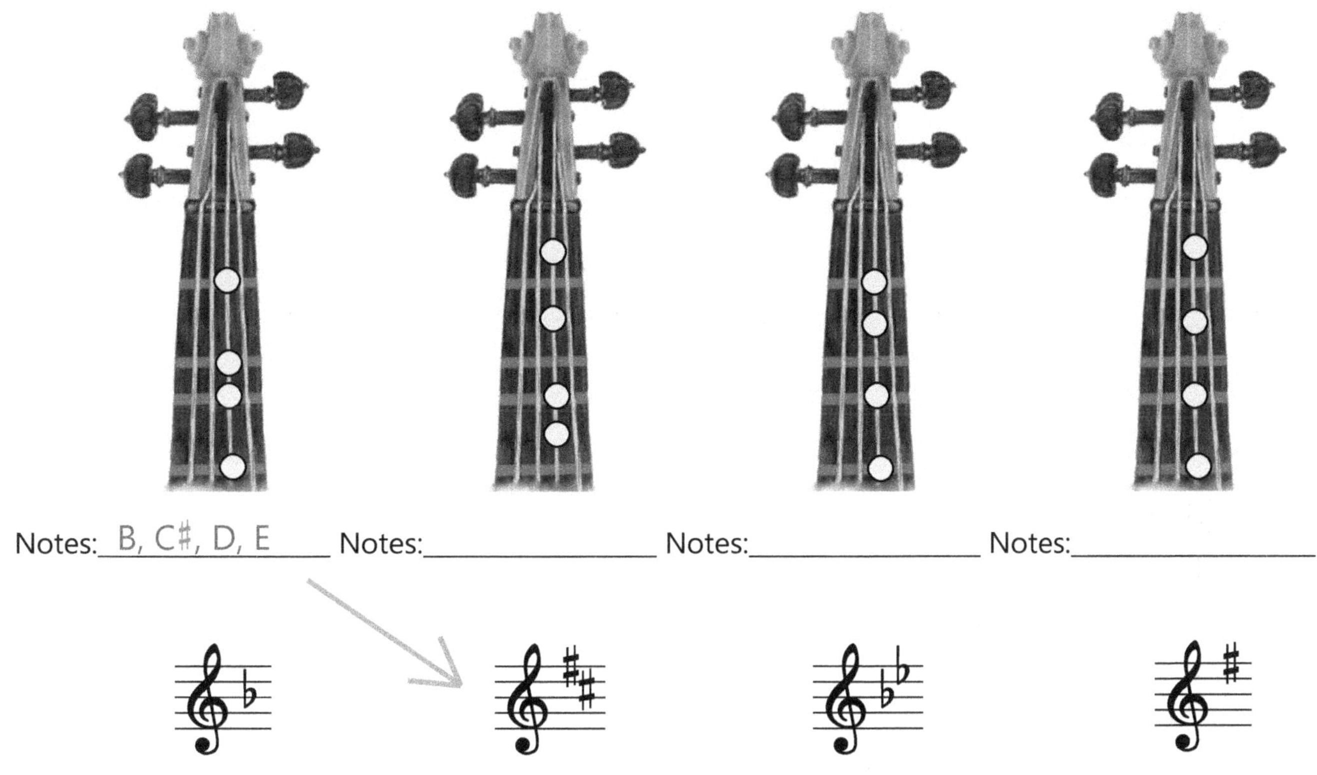


Draw the finger pattern on the D string for the following key signatures:

1. 
2. 
3. 
4. 

Sharps/Flats: B♭, E♭ Sharps/Flats:__________ Sharps/Flats:__________ Sharps/Flats:__________

1. 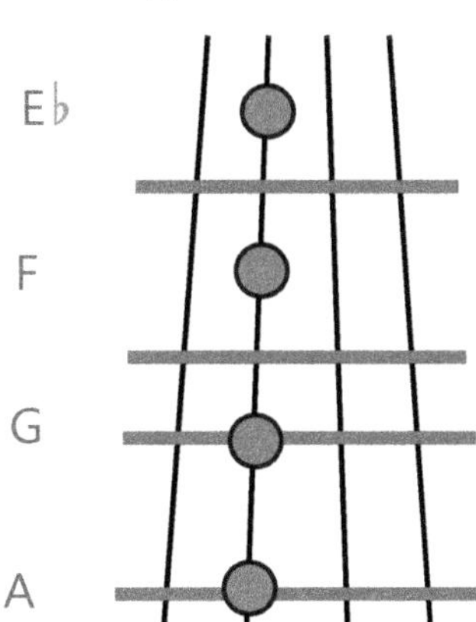

2. 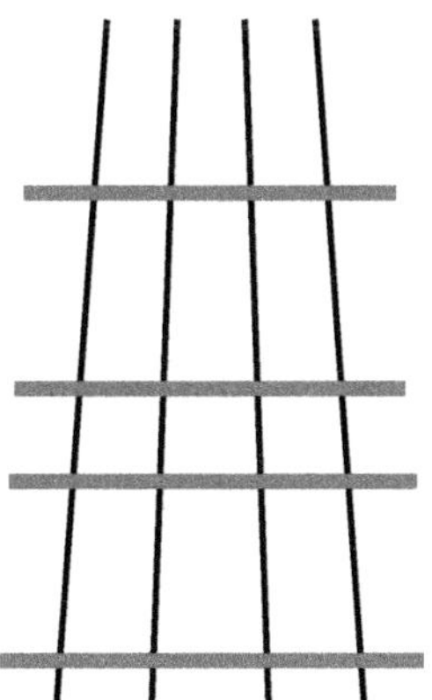
3. 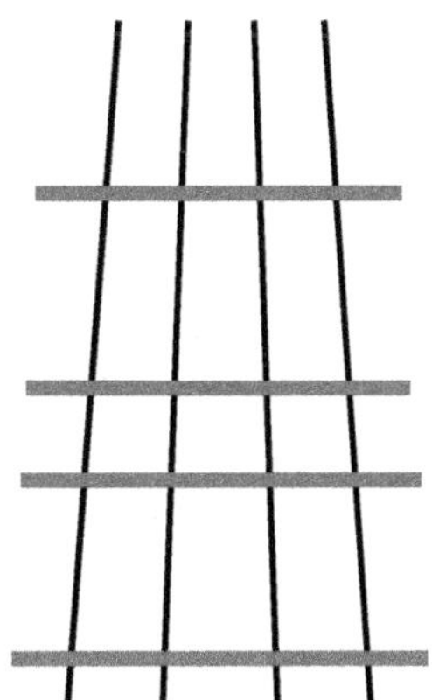
4. 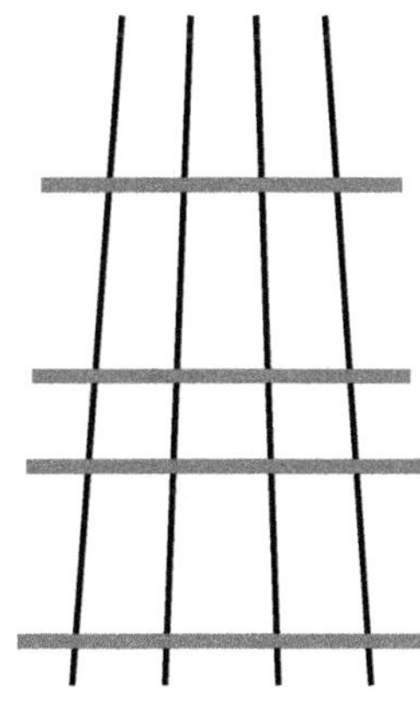

# Advanced Scales

Label all of the notes in each scale using finger numbers and letter names. Then draw the location of the notes on the violin.

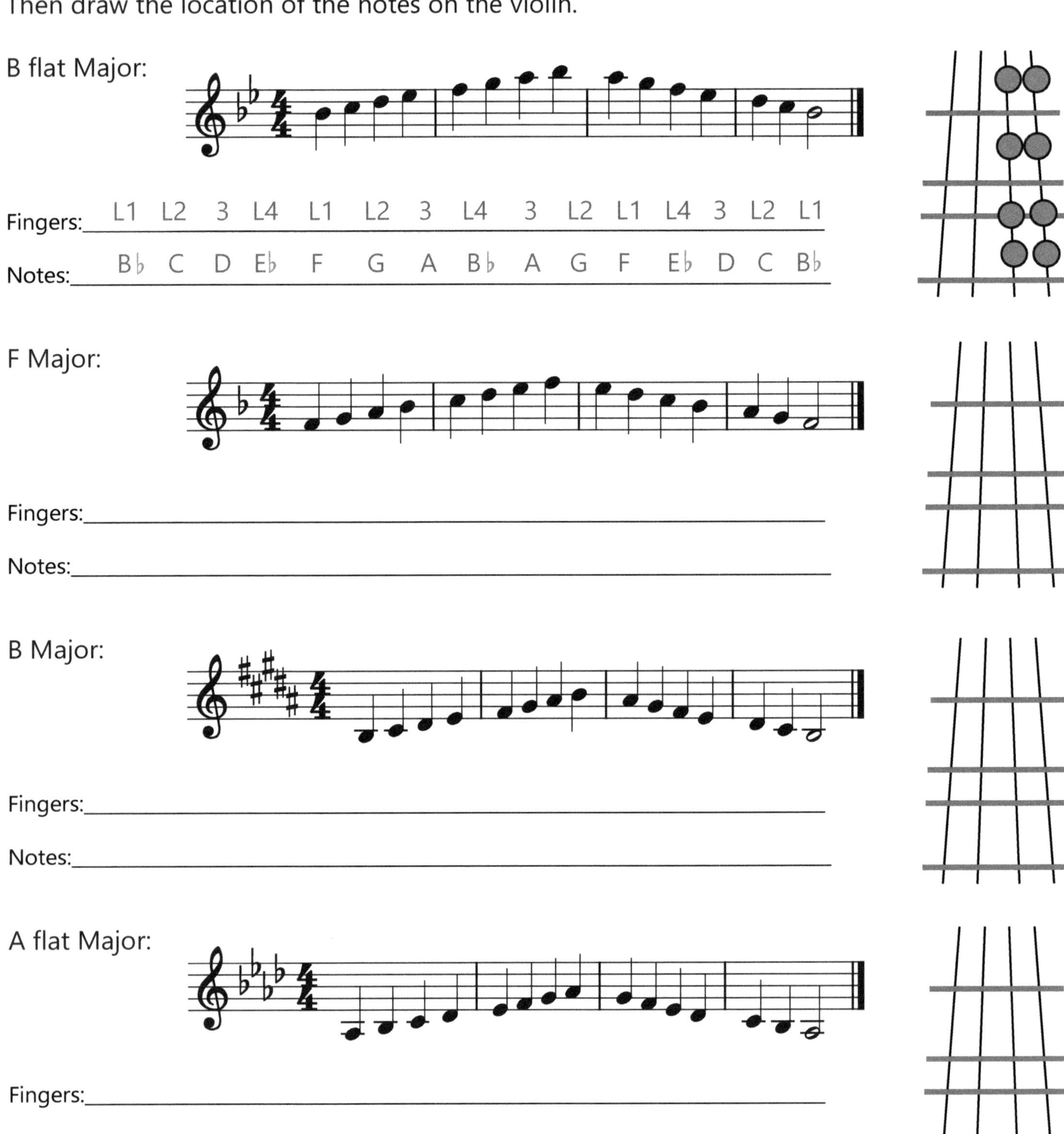

# Say and Play 2 Octave Scales

Think about how the key signature affects the finger patterns.

G major

A major

Bb major

Ab major

B major

www.ingramcontent.com/pod-product-compliance
Lightning Source LLC
LaVergne TN
LVHW070937160826
845679LV00021B/1829

*9798990505308*